Psychologists With No God

ALBERT TALKER

© Copyright 2015, Albert Talker

All rights reserved.

No portion of this book may be reproduced, stored in a retrieval system, or transmitted in any form or by means—electronic, mechanical, photocopy, recording, scanning, or other excerpt for brief quotations in critical reviews or articles, without prior written permission of the publisher.

ISBN: 978-1-60414-892-3

All characters appearing in this work are fictitious. Any resemblance to real persons, living or dead is purely coincidental. Places and locations narrated in this work are fictitious. Any resemblance to real location or place is purely coincidental.

This novel is dedicated to all the tens of millions of fathers in the Western World who will never see their children again, and to the thousands of men and women who lost their lives due to sicknesses during and after divorce because of this highly emotional and adversarial process. This book is also dedicated to the millions of children who grew up and will grow up without fathers.

Contents

CHAPTER ONE	Single Again	1
CHAPTER TWO	Psychologists with no God	9
CHAPTER THREE	Judge Irish and Court Proceedings	12
CHAPTER FOUR	Family Court Without a Lawyer	18
CHAPTER FIVE	The Restraining Order	28
CHAPTER SIX	The Trial	38
CHAPTER SEVEN	Meeting Maya	49
CHAPTER EIGHT	Early Days	55
CHAPTER NINE	Early Married Life	59
CHAPTER TEN	Trial Continues	70
CHAPTER ELEVEN	The Terror	119
CHAPTER TWELVE	Maya's Affair	124
CHAPTER THIRTEEN	Dr. Psylie, Court Appointed Custody Evaluator	129
CHAPTER FOURTEEN	Dr. Psylie — Second Appointment	137
CHAPTER FIFTEEN	Mr. Muller — Court Appointed Reunification Therapist	143
CHAPTER SIXTEEN	Early Military Life	148
CHAPTER SEVENTEEN	Guilty	153
CHAPTER EIGHTEEN	The Arrest	168

CHAPTER NINETEEN	The Love Party	172
CHAPTER TWENTY	Maya and Dr. Rosensthal	176
CHAPTER TWENTY-ONE	Ally's Inheritance	184

APPENDIX

- Issues Raised in this Book 195
- Fatherless Nation Statistics 199
- Child Support Stats 203
- Facts Regarding False Accusations of Abuse 204
- Fatherless Nation — The Effects 205

CHAPTER ONE

Single Again

It was an exceptionally beautiful spring morning in mid-April, the kind that makes the darkness and cold of winter hide in shame. I had a breakfast of coffee and toast, dressed for work and left the apartment I was living in at the Delta Complex in Aberdeen, New Jersey.

As I walked slowly toward my car, engulfed in my thoughts, I narrowly avoided colliding with my neighbor on the sidewalk. She wished me a good morning, and I wished her the same. Glancing towards the swimming pool, I hoped to catch a glimpse of the young Hungarian lifeguard. This woman provided me with some company during swimming practice in this lonely apartment complex. Each time I saw her, she displayed a happy smile, mixed with some curiosity and caution.

I sometimes felt ashamed for having feelings for this young lady who looked on me as a fatherly friend. I didn't know her name. I passed next to the fence surrounding the pool, but she wasn't there.

Suddenly I got a tremendous jolt of euphoria as I realized it was April 18, my birthday. Somehow it had slipped my mind.

Driving toward work I looked at the bright cloudless sky and realized that this Friday was going to be a wonderful day. Some of the pink and white blossoms on the trees had started to dress in green again, as fresh leaves joined the flowers on the limbs. It gave me a sense of renewal, looking at the spring coming to cheer us after the long winter.

In the last several months I was so absorbed in myself, so isolated from my family, I was crushed just thinking what had happened to me.

I even gave up attending evening classes in writing. I was jarred out of my melancholy thoughts by the sudden shrill but merry tune of my cellphone, and I eagerly answered the call. It was my mother calling from Florida. She gave me best wishes for my birthday, and asked about her grandchildren. I told her that I saw them so seldom; I wasn't sure how they were doing.

"Don't worry, children are resilient!" she said, knowing how much I worried about them witnessing their parents' messy divorce, their lack of a father at home, just as my own father had been largely absent even when present in the flesh.

The emotional costs of my failed marriage had been gradually sinking in, and I realized that Maya, my wife, made me feel that I was the main reason for this failure. What Maya instilled in me was the sense that I lacked communication skills with all women, and that I would fail with any other I might marry. At the time I really believed her. I knew that Maya has issues emanating from her battered childhood, but I was still convinced it was me that caused this failure. I also knew that Maya perceived my good nature as stupidity and my kindness as a weakness, and I couldn't understand why.

I couldn't bear the thought of my children living there with Maya, unable to visit me, or perhaps they didn't want to see me, or any other man with their mother. I remembered when I had dated divorced women, the faces of their children when I arrived for a date made me uneasy. I would not take other men's children under my protection, simply because I wasn't their father and their father existed somewhere. I couldn't envision this situation with my children, and I also knew that there are many men who prey on divorced women, many of whom are starved for love, companionship, and a new relationship. As my wife had engaged in an affair while we were married, I figured she would not hold back with me out of the house. But I couldn't bear the thought that my wife and children would live this life style.

Driving towards my train station I passed by the Marlboro Elementary School, where my two daughters were enrolled. Watching the children play, I felt suddenly that I needed to see them. I called Anika, my youngest daughter, and said I was on the way to the house to see them for a few minutes before they go to school.

Even though I had a restraining order against me that forbade me from approaching the house except at visitation times, my urge to see them was irresistible. I felt elated and happy, but I could feel the strange tightening of the muscles in my stomach and my racing pulse, which happened every time I drove close to my house.

This time, however, the pain was unbearable, as my body had already surrendered to pancreatic cancer for which I elected to forgo treatments. Standing outside, on the front steps of my house — the house that was no longer legally mine or ours — I reached out and knocked several faint knocks on the door.

Anika opened the door and jumped to me full of joy, screaming, "Papa, Papa, I love you!" I hugged her tightly and kissed her and told her that I love her very much. When my oldest daughter, Ally, approached the open door and saw me there, she got startled and called her mother. Maya's hostility toward me was raging again, as she approached me and asked me to leave immediately. She threatened to call the police and have me put again in jail.

Last weekend's experience of being locked up for the night on a false accusation of a restraining order violation was an experience I wanted to forget, and never repeat. Just thinking about it sent chills down my spine. She saw that I was startled by the threat, and being a psychologist who knew me well, decided it would be best to calm me down. After all, I was still paying all my obligations, which would be at risk if I were locked up.

She then said in a gentler tone that the kids had to go to school and she had to prepare for work. Her career had always been her priority, and nothing could stand in her way. But when she asked me to leave again, to my surprise both Ally and Anika hugged me tightly and barely let me go.

When I turned to go my youngest cried out, "Papa, don't go! Papa, please don't leave!" Heartbroken, I forced myself to leave anyway. I didn't want Maya to yell at me again or call the police, which she did with regularity.

Waving goodbye at the front door, now closing shut with more force than necessary, I decided to skip work and drive to my favorite airport.

The Farmingdale Airport was a remnant of World War II, situated in what is now a largely industrial region. I liked taking off from their longest runway, as I could fly low over it, gaining speed and quickly raising the nose to climb fast.

I left my car unlocked and left a note to my children saying that I loved them.

I suddenly felt the urge to cry, and childhood memories came flooding back to me. One of the strangest images was that of my father, whom I never saw cry. I had witnessed my mother cry and yell many times, but never my father. I couldn't understand why I could cry when I couldn't see my children, yet my father never cried and didn't care whether he saw his children or not.

He did work hard to provide for his family and showed some vague signs that he cared for us, though. It seemed to me the older generations were brought up this way. I have learned that those childhood memories effected on my personality and how I conduct myself, a lesson in avoiding the negatives — I would not do as he had done, I would avoid being like him in any way.

I had learned the most intense and horrific lesson in the last year, also something I glimpsed from childhood; There is a delicate line between sanity and insanity, good and bad, innocence and guilt, loyalty and betrayal, health and sickness, and between life and death. That delicate line can easily be crossed. I looked at myself, comprehending that a healthy mind needs a healthy body, and that my subconscious had been tainted by my own deeds and my sick body giving up its battle. *If this is God's will, so be it,* I thought.

I walked towards my chosen plane, an older model Piper Cherokee with one engine and four seats. It always gave me great pleasure to fly this bird. It stood there shining in the sun, looking like a big streamlined white car with large silver wings. I always admired the beauty of airplanes, and I could find personality in each one. They are all wild, these dazzling flying beasts, and need to be carefully controlled — for they could also kill.

I knew how to fly well, just as I knew every inch of this bird. I thoroughly checked out the Cherokee and climbed into the cockpit. I started the engine and checked the instruments, skipping no procedure. I always went by the book. I fondled the yoke and turned on all the required switches. Yes, I was sure — almost sure — I was perfectly safe in this plane.

Almost irrationally, I started listing in my head the reasons why this airplane was safe: It had a single engine — no need to worry about changing pitch or controlling multiple engines. It had fixed landing gear, and the steel framework of this plane was made of was built to last.

The airport was self-announcing, in that it didn't have an active control tower. I declared into the microphone that I was taking off from Runway 32, and proceeded as usual. I hugged the runway as much as I could before suddenly pulling back the yoke. Then the airplane's nose lifted up and accelerated towards the sky. After several minutes of being in the air, I declared my intentions: "Farmingdale executive, Piper Cherokee, after takeoff from Runway 32, turning right departing to the North."

No one was in the vicinity and I couldn't hear anyone else in the pattern. I enjoyed the view and was flying with calm confidence. The sky was cloudless and the view was unlimited. I could see Manhattan Island, but with the Twin Towers gone, Manhattan was less recognizable. The Twin Towers had been a reference beacon for every pilot flying in the area.

My memory of the buildings going down made me think again of my childhood, for I suddenly started uttering a prayer that I'd known all my life. My grandfather always repeated this prayer, God rest his soul. I didn't know why I was saying this prayer again and again, but I noticed I was flying toward the home that once was mine.

"Please, listen to me, God of the Universe, our God, and God of all. Blessed be thy kingdom forever and ever. Please listen to me God of the Universe, our God, and God of all. Blessed be thy kingdom forever and ever. Please listen to me God of the Universe, our God, and God of all. Blessed be thy kingdom forever and ever!"

I thought I heard a faint voice inside the aircraft, but it wasn't one of the controllers calling me on the radio and it wasn't coming through my earphones. Without hearing any actual words, I responded, listening to myself talking as if from a distance: "I want to know why God created the universe, Earth, and man. I want to know why He made us smart enough to learn his ways and understand his powers, but evil enough to create pain, sorrow and mayhem."

Yes, this was the question that plagued so many believers who couldn't comprehend why such a supreme power would allow such suffering on this earth, the world that was often a hell for most people, only occasionally giving the taste of a heavenly realm.

Something made me think of the manuscript that my spouse had submitted to the court to remove me from the house in which we had lived with our children. Why did she do such an unethical deed? I couldn't figure out the judge's actions, suspending my child visitations based on those pages.

It was a private, therapeutic writing between my therapist and me. Why did he take it so seriously? Did the first amendment of free speech and doctor-patient confidentiality go out the window when any threatening fantasy surfaced?

Looking out at the world below me, I could see the New Jersey Parkway in the distance. I had begun to start flying towards my house during my musing and mumbling, but couldn't put the two together — the direction of my flight and the problem with that manuscript. I continued flying, saying things under my breath such as, "Man has always been conscious of the existence of a Supreme Being, the Master and Creator of all, blessed be thy kingdom forever and ever, hear me Father." It was as if my mind was splitting in two, the side that talked to God, and the other that talked to myself.

Suddenly I saw a flash of bright white light in front of me, and I again heard that deep voice, only this time it said, *"You are diagnosed with ter-*

minal cancer and you should not fly!" I looked around and checked my earphones, but they were plugged and my radio was silent.

"I want to. My children are lost to me. I have no family. What is there to live for? Everything is gone. I'll die very soon anyway. Slowly and painfully, I'll not be able to hide my disease much longer."

"Satan also rules in my universe, and evil is Satan's lot," the voice answered.

"Please forgive me I'm turning back now," I whispered.

The bright light before me started to fade away, and with it went the voice. I could now only hear the engine running and radio noise in my earphones. I was terrified. I didn't know if I was hallucinating or losing it. I knew that I never hallucinated, or had even been close to really losing my mind. The voice and light wasn't an illusion, but more of a breakthrough to another level of communication and insight — that I was sure of. In my uncertainty, I began to feel calm and started humming the Queen's song as I did in battle 25 years ago —

> *Without you, when you're gone*
> *You took me for everything that I had,*
> *And kicked me out on my own.*

I was now flying over my old neighborhood, executing a low turning dive so that I could be sure my children had left for school and my wife had gone to work. There was no car in the driveway, but I called the house several times to be certain no one was there.

> *There are plenty of ways you can hurt a man*
> *And bring him to the ground.*

I circled my house again and positioned myself to make the sort of bombing run I had been trained for. The airplane was still shaking from the steep turn I was making, and I was pushing the throttles to full power to start the dive.

Suddenly I felt pain rushing through my body into my head and I knew it was the pain of cancer without medication. The airplane vibrated and the air passing over the wings whistled. For the first time in my life I passed the speed limit set for any airplane, causing a tremendous noise to emanate from the body of the craft. The smell of burnt oil and rubber came to me as drops of engine sprayed onto my windscreen.

I could see my house approaching quickly, and my instincts told me *Pull-up! Pull-up! Pull-up! Pull-up!* But I didn't. I lost consciousness and the Piper Cherokee hit a large concrete parking lot in a park-like area not far from my house at 9:30 on that glorious morning. It disintegrated into thousands of shiny pieces mixed with blood and bone. Nothing was left of me to bury.

The part of my brain that still cherished my body continued to feel. I was still flying my burning plane, though I could see and hear nothing. I tried to shout, I tried to speak, but I couldn't. Then I tried to wave my hands before accepting I didn't have a body.

Suddenly someone was speaking to me, but they were inside my mind, *"The universe consists of a series of events stretched across time in a long causal chain. Each one of these events is the cause of the event that comes after it, and the effect of the event that comes before it."*

Then, there before me was the same bright white light I'd seen before, and it was approaching me. Within seconds I was completely taken into its calm and welcoming radiance.

CHAPTER TWO

Psychologists with No God

My name is David. I have always been clear minded, correct in my thoughts, and I've never tried drugs, alcohol or tobacco. I have always followed the law and never got into trouble. I come from many generations of Free Masons, and I keep to the high moral ground I was taught to maintain. I believe in love, family, and living with honor, as well as telling the truth. But, things were happening to me that upset all my convictions and values.

I was living alone in my apartment now, not far away from my family — the family that now lived without me. I had been diagnosed with pancreatic cancer recently, and that was ultimately a death sentence. I had attributed the abdominal pain, depression and loss of appetite that I had been experiencing to my recent problems, and had ignored the symptoms for much too long. Now the disease was at an advanced stage.

I was devastated when my illness was eventually diagnosed, but chose not to go through any treatments. I always thought that part of the medical system resembled the judicial system — doctors, like lawyers, seem to recommend expensive and often hopeless treatments that do little more than increase suffering and accelerate the inevitable. That just wasn't for me.

My doctor explained that my disease was fast growing and usually returns even when it is operable. Not that this stopped him from recommending a range of useless treatments.

I didn't tell anyone about my prognosis. What was the point? My psychologist wife, who initiated divorce proceedings after starting an affair with her college mentor, would not care. She doesn't want or need me anymore. She'll probably celebrate me being out their lives.

My two daughters were surprised and shocked by the sudden break up of our family. Telling them this news would only make their lives feel more unstable.

It seemed like the divorce wasn't only a surprise for me, it was like a death sentence itself. I was upset and worried about my children's future. Now, they would have to live without a father who loved them. It already seemed like it was too late for eleven-year-old Ally, who has a severe case of Parental Alienation Syndrome (PAS). This usually happens in child custody cases, where the litigating parent hopes to gain leverage in court or at home by programming the child against the other parent. Ally completely rejects my visitations, refusing to see me during the few times I have been able to meet with my family.

Living as a single man is completely different from when I was young. That was a time when most men chose to get married and keep the family together at all costs. Now it's like my family doesn't exist anymore. I have children but I can't see them. What's worse is that they've been brainwashed by their mother into thinking I didn't love them or have their interests in mind.

I had a lawyer who represented me for many months during the divorce proceedings, but he didn't help. Since I was out of our marital house over 15 months before the divorce, because my spouse had accused me of being dangerous to the children, the court stopped my visitations with them. I ran out of funds to defend my rights to see my Ally and Anika, and I was contemplating options to fold up and go to another country so I could start a new life. What was this life without my children?

But now, I was near broke. Several months after the dismissal of my lawyer, I could no longer afford legal representation. My spouse, Maya, however, had a real bloodhound to represent her. She was a good judge of character, and knew this lawyer would suit her needs.

The one pleasure left to me, my true love, was flying. It was a something I could control, that didn't turn on me — or so I thought. I needed this hobby. It calmed and relaxed me, while thrilling me at the same time. I had been an airman for seven years, and now I could enjoy it as a sport, at my leisure. I'd go rising into the skies with fewer cares than a bird. Looking down at the landscape, the buildings, cars and houses, the tiny people no bigger than ants, time itself seemed to lose its power, and my problems diminished.

The expansiveness of the sky seemed to be my real playing field, one closer to God than any piece of earth to inhabit. But when I landed again, and got into my car to get back on the highway toward my little apartment near but so far from my lost family, my situation came crashing back to me.

When I entered my home, it was the same as when I left — silent and static. Nothing had moved since I was there last. The cup I had left in the sink was still in the same spot. There was no sound of children and no warmth of family. Looking out the windows I could see no future for myself. Turning in the direction of the home that was once mine, I wondered what my family was doing, those three generations of women under one roof, with no man.

After weeks of this, I started avoiding coming home at night, and would stay longer in the restaurants I frequented. I came to know the staff in many of those places and they were kind, perhaps sensing that I was a lonely divorced man. I met other men in my same situation when I dined out, and we all harbored feelings of anger and resentment. We all had similar problems with the family court, our ex-wives and the legal system. Usually our conversations turned into angry confessions, telling stories that seemed to have many common threads.

CHAPTER THREE

Judge Irish and Court Proceedings

After Maya filed for divorce, Judge Irish was assigned to our case. Initially I didn't face the judge, as there was no need to meet him because my lawyer handled things. The divorce process initially went smoothly.

I first faced Judge Irish when I had a court hearing at Monmouth regarding my visitation rights and the fact that the opposing counsel had requested they be suspended because was "dangerous to the children." This determination was made based on a manuscript I had written with my therapist. My spouse had picked it up off my printer, just before I moved out of our home. I was surprised that a document used in therapy could be used to determine the author was "dangerous." It seemed silly to me, since I'd spent 10 years day and night with my children.

They say everything is possible in America, and at that point I was starting to believe it. The Monmouth courthouse was located in Freehold, New Jersey — the town where "Born in the USA" singer Bruce Springsteen was born and raised. How ironic, I thought while standing in front of the big building. I was born in the USA, and so were my children. And there I was, at the beginning of my experience with this famous justice system, thinking about Springsteen's sarcastic words that questioned so-called American values versus their actions. I was humming his song as I approached the security guard at the courthouse.

"Please leave your bags on the belt," the security officer said distractedly, as he let me go through. I imagined all the distressed fathers, mothers and other family members he had seen entering this door, and I assumed that he was used to seeing the various expressions and moods people display when entering this courthouse. I asked him for directions to the courtroom and he pointed me in the right direction.

Judge Irish's courtroom looked like a big classroom, with a stage of chairs and tables where the judge's comfortable chair rose above all. *Yes, he has the king's seat,* I was thinking, *"while I'm just the simple peasant coming to hear his decision."* I sat, uncomfortably on my wooden chair, while Judge Irish made us wait. I learned that most people spend the majority of their time just waiting when they were in court, just watching the clock tick away all the money they were paying their lawyers.

After about 20 minutes we finally heard, "All rise! Honorable Judge Irish presiding." We all stood as the king of the courtroom entered and signaled the beginning of the court's busy day. I stared quietly at Judge Irish, as did the rest of the people in the courtroom. He was a man in his early 60s, who was nearly bald with a totally perfect round face. He looked a bit dazed, as if he wasn't quite ready for the day. I felt the same way.

We all were allowed to take our seats as the assistant to the judge started calling the cases one by one. In the meantime, all the pending cases had to wait for their arbitrarily selected turn. The minutes dragged by.

When the master of ceremonies decided to take a break, stepping into his chambers behind the courtroom stage, my lawyer and I took the opportunity for a short brief. It was clear he was still studying the case, and didn't grasp the depths my spouse was going to. I wondered if he worried that I didn't have enough money to afford his representation.

I worried that he wasn't up to the job. Maya had a better lawyer, one that could easily lie in court and stand by her client's lies without raising any doubts. I had heard that her lawyer knew how to play the game better.

"All Rise!" the court guard yelled as the grim-faced judge returned to the podium. The guy never smiled, not even a half-smile. Staring at his stern expression, I had a strange feeling that things might not go my way today.

I was startled as I heard the court guard suddenly yell, "Maya vs. David Tal!" I instinctively got up and followed my lawyer's steps. The court guard ordered us to pass through the small wooden gate and take our seats in front of the judge. My lawyer led me to take the seat next to him in front of the judge's podium, while Maya was positioned to our left with her lawyer.

Judge Irish started: "This is the case of Tal vs. Tal." He read from the motion notes filed by my spouse's lawyer, which were basically asking that I not be allowed to see my children because I was dangerous. I had served as an Air-Force officer, and I had written a manuscript in therapy that proved I was unstable and dangerous.

Furthermore, the opposing lawyer was requesting more support money and an increase in the child support payments than had already been decided several months earlier. My lawyer, Mr. Rosen, fell silent but remained standing. He had tried to object in his loud high-pitched voice using simple terms, unlike my spouse's lawyer who used double-edged words with multiple meanings, almost like she talked from both sides of her mouth at once.

My inept lawyer paused every so often and looked at the judge as though waiting for his approval, then he shot a glance at me. His expression was clear — just sit quietly with your mouth closed.

After my lawyer finished his response, Judge Irish spoke in a tone that seemed considerate and sincere. "The priority of the court isn't to disrupt a father's relationship with his children."

I looked at the judge with a great sense of suspicion. *Does he really mean what he just said?* I wondered.

Then he turned to my lawyer and using a critical tone advised him to listen carefully, "Your client's case is one I must think twice about before writing my orders. Your client is accused of being unstable and dangerous to the children. This is a serious allegation."

My lawyer jumped and cried out, "Your Honor!"

The Judge ignored Mr. Rosen and addressed Ms. Mussolini, my spouse's counsel, asking for her side of the story.

"Your Honor, the Defendant has provided the court with a letter from her husband's therapist, Ms. Mally, stating that he doesn't suffer from depression and she doesn't see him as a danger to his children or anyone else. This conclusion is based on her observations and therapy sessions."

"What's your point?" Judge Irish responded.

"To be certain on this point, I would request a risk assessment for the defendant and until such time he should not be able to see his children," Ms. Mussolini responded.

I shook my head in disbelief before standing up and responding, against my lawyer's advice.

"Your Honor, that letter stated several issues about me that somehow the opposing lawyer wants to disregard. My therapist, Ms. Mally, also said that my pilot's license is clean, my credit records are clean, I've never had a police record, my driving record is clean, and I was never involved in even one traffic violation. I served with honor in the Air Force and then later worked on top security research projects. I got drunk or got into bad situations, never tried drugs and never had any adulterous affairs. She said I have demonstrated a record of stability and responsibility and she doesn't understand why I have to go through this process in order to get visitation!"

"So what," the judge responded angrily, staring at me in disbelief, "you want to represent himself now?"

"Okay! I give up!" I shouted as I went back to my seat. I had broken the rules. I knew I was supposed to let my lawyer speak for me, but he seemed so helpless. I just couldn't stop myself. I saw my spouse and her lawyer grinning and knew I'd' done more damage than good. I also realized she would do anything to keep me away from our children — even if she had to use every dirty trick possible to achieve this goal. This judge, that lawyer, this lie, that half-truth, and I was banned legally from seeing my children!

"What has happened here?" I asked in a bewildered voice.

Mr. Rosen didn't volunteer further information about what was happening, "It is what it is, and the Judge has ruled," he replied briefly and sarcastically. "What did you expect after that outburst? They've entered your response into the court proceeding, now you really don't have any chance for visitations with your children now that you've made the judge angry. The judge doesn't like to hear from anyone but the lawyers in his courtroom."

Mr. Rosen didn't admit to his lack of representation and the offensive attitude Maya's lawyer had taken. It seemed like there was no truth, only ego battles between lawyers in this case, and the lawyer who could lie better had won. It didn't matter that my children were the ultimate losers.

Mr. Rosen looked grave and serious as he admonished me, "You *cannot* see your children until you get a risk assessment. We will meet again after you get the assessment."

"Forty percent of American men do not see their children after divorce and now I know why," I responded to my counsel. "Most men cannot afford the legal battle and the heavy child support payments, so they withdraw from the battle. Today is another testament to what's happening in family court, and it is massive child abduction in this fatherless nation!" My counsel looked at me with a sad smile, and left the room without uttering any further word.

Reality hit me hard as I realized I was completely alone. I wouldn't be seeing my children for many months to come. Thinking about what had just happened, I wrote the following poem summarizing my experience:

Father's Visitation Rights

Between sundown and nightfall,
When father's rights for visitation approach,
Love crept along in the shadows,
And the sheltering hope was left behind.

That precious time known as visitation,
Was swept away in a blind rage,
Costing the children's fatherly hours,
Now he's left alone in the angry rage.

High up in the lonely skies,
A disappointed father watched and waited,
Evil beasts in every corner,
He was stunned and disappointed but never blinded.

Wolves hiding behind every bush,
Need to come to a pause in the day's manifest,
That wolf and man are brothers,
When it comes to the Children's hours.

CHAPTER FOUR

Family Court Without a Lawyer

I decided to change my situation but I didn't know how. I wasn't seeing my children, my legal bills were escalating and no hope was in sight. Fall had just crept in to crisp the air and color the leaves of the maples and oaks. Bright reds, oranges and yellows mocked my sadness and made me think of a more hopeful time when we'd just moved to "the garden state."

On that beautiful day nearing the peak of fall color, I drove to my flying club, Eagles-Eye Aviation. It looked like a Second World War squadron building, located on the northern side of the runway, where planes took off and landed. I entered and looked at the airplanes parked and tied down within the fenced area. The club owners required them to be tied to the ground, even if left for a short time. It seemed as if they thought the planes might take flight on their own. They certainly looked capable of it, sitting with noses facing forward and wings ready.

I'd belonged to this club for many years, but this sight always awed me a little. I adored looking at the dozen or so aircraft, all painted in bright colors and in different in interesting ways. For me, this was a vision that was more enjoyable than any other scenic view on earth.

Pamela, one of the club owners, was standing behind the desk when I approached. "Hi David. What's up?"

"Do you have the Piper warrior available?"

Pamela nodded and said, "Yes, it will be ready in about half an hour."

I headed to the back of the training room. It had large windows with no drapes or shades on them. The room was always filled with light on sunny days..

Pamela looked at me with sympathy. "I heard you're going through a divorce," she said in a gentle tone.

"Yes, I am — a bad one," I admitted, trying not to sound too bitter.

"Excuse me for speaking up, but I see you as a friend, David, a part of our family here. You might want to talk to Vince Newbank, one of our top instructors. He has experience with the divorce process. He did it all successfully, without lawyers, and he's a very good man. He cares about others and his students love him. He has some down time now, no one in for another half hour," she added, glancing up at the wall clock. She then pointed to where the flight instructor sat at his desk in the far corner.

Feeling optimistic, I approached Vince to see if he was willing to talk to me about such a personal matter. Someone who had beaten the Goliath would be a good advisor to this David. He was about my age, neatly groomed and dressed in a conservative blue tie and shirt, black pants, short haircut. He had a narrow, almost child-like face and wore an expression of openness. I remembered him from previous trips to the club, and recalled that he smiled a lot.

Vince rose from his chair and smiled as he approached. He shook my hand and I could see his smile hid some pain or bitterness he wasn't quite able to mask. Right away I thought of Vince as another lonely man who could help me with my legal troubles. Maybe he'd lost his children's hearts and company to a mean-spirited spouse as well.

And while this man who beat the legal system at its own game was a winner, he seemed to have little happiness in his victory. His family was still broken.

As we began to talk, I was pleased that his warmth and concern for others extended to me. I felt as if we were members of the divorced father's club. After I briefly described my situation and the endless battles my spouse was initiating with her unscrupulous lawyer, I became aware of his vast knowledge in family law.

As it turned out, he was the first one to win litigation against his ex-wife for inducing parental alienation in their children in the state of New Jersey. When he offered to help me in handling my divorce, I felt surely he was my man.

I listened as he described what happens to some men in these circumstances; how their spouses' lawyers act when they think you have money and equity in the marital house. They often cause problems to the opposing counsel just to please their vengeful client and thus bill them for their unnecessary bullying actions. Many of them promise their clients a great deal just to satisfy their clients' need for revenge for reasons only God knows, and then file endless motions just to justify their billing, while their gullible clients just go deeper into debt. While these details were disturbing, I wasn't surprised, for I had seen some of this abuse at the hands of my own lawyer. I figured there had to be another way to do this.

"I'm terminating my lawyer today!" I said dramatically. "He's joining my wife's lawyer in some macabre dance of motions, trials and accusations. And he bills me just for stirring up trouble!" My emotions had been bottled up for such a long time; I couldn't help but let them loose when facing this sympathetic man.

"You may want to weigh your options here. I'd be glad to help you," Vince said. "Just don't act hastily. You need to have a plan if you're going to handle it yourself, as going pro-se isn't easy. You know all aspects of the case better than anyone else, whereas a lawyer can only do so much on your behalf. But you must make this choice. I can only advise you."

"Your airplane is here!" I heard Pamela yell from the end of the room.

"Thank you, Vince! I'll talk to you soon about this." I shook his hand and went off to fly on one of my favorite airplanes, the Piper Warrior. It had a long, sleek body of blue and cream, and smooth lines from tip to tail, and it was easy to fly and maneuver. I needed this hobby. It calmed and relaxed me, while thrilling me at the same time. In the cockpit I felt I really was an eagle flying over the land below, that I really was leading a warrior that would come to my aid as a trust between the sacred bird, the great symbol of the United States, and its fierce love of freedom.

During the next few days after I met Vince, I weighed the issue of whether to go pro-se. *Can I really handle this?* I wondered. *Is it too much of a risk to go against the grain, to go alone?* With the image of Vince in my mind, a regular man like myself who had decided to trust himself, I figured that with his help, I was capable of writing motions to the court, thus representing myself before the judge and the opposing counsel.

It was a strange period of peace and hopefulness during those few weeks, especially after feeling so helpless against the system. Though I had some doubts from time to time about my course of action, I finally decided it was the right thing to do.

I felt better immediately, perhaps for several reasons. I would take things into my own hands, and get to know "the enemy." I had no lawyer to defend me, but no one was billing me either. The fog that my spouse's lawyer had wrapped over Maya and me, from which she had no escape, no longer clouded me. I was now the fog maker, in the driver's seat, not some stranger who pretended to defend me but had no interest outside of money.

I had relied on lawyers for advice and direction, yet I still had some trouble accepting the fact that they could do little to help me under the circumstances. I knew many lawyers just bill and bill, file motions and send letters, like an endless macabre dance of a dog chasing its tail. The best lawyer in town would've had problems following the rapid chain of events that happened in this divorce. Nobody could really understand it unless they spent more time on my case than any of us could afford. Only my spouse and I knew the real circumstances, while the rest was all a stage act, or in my case, a horror show.

Now I was determined to spend what time I had to learn how to respond to the legal system, with a new bible to learn, one I slept with every night, on my table next to the bed. The *New Jersey Family Law* book had over 1000 pages, but I found ways to glance through it quickly and locate chapters, cases and laws that pertained to my case. Vince had given me several sample motions he had filed, along with instructions on how to proceed and prepare the motions. His advice gave me good overview on how to stand for myself in the court and its legalities. "There is nothing more to lose," I told myself calmly, holding onto my thoughts of "I can do it."

From the time I left my home and went off to live by myself, the normal working of my mind seemed to be flawed. My confidence in myself and my abilities, even though established in my personality and self-awareness, could be undermined by a single thought of that bloodhound on my trail. The loss of my children never seemed to stop hurting.

What did I do to make this happen? I wondered. *Is it my fault? Did my intense love for Maya make me blind to her true personality?* My main fear in going forward on my own was that Maya's lawyer would see me as vulnerable without legal help, and try to stop any chances of me getting visitation.

I also worried that the bank accounts Maya and her family kept secret would allow her to lie about her resources outside my support. I just hated the deceit and lies that were forming like a fence to keep me out, emotionally, professionally, and financially.

In the rough draft of my legal document, my first motion to the family court, I asked for an investigation of bank accounts my spouse held with her mother and sister, visitation rights with my youngest daughter and an experienced therapist for my oldest daughter, who suffered with an advanced state of Parental Alienation Syndrome.

When I called Vince to set an appointment to finalize my first motion to the court, he again came to my aid with the same friendliness he had first shown me at the club. Visiting my home at night, he asked me where I stood with the process.

"I'm trying my best," I told him, putting my paperwork before him. "But I need to pick your brain again."

Vince looked down at the papers and said, "Okay, I'll let you pick my brain, but first I need you to listen. Actually, it would be best to write down some notes. I'll make some statements and you need to write it down, okay?" I watched him for a few moments as he skimmed through the first pages of my draft that outlined my wife's situation and actions, and the steps leading up to the divorce. Then he straightened himself in his chair and said "Time to get to this business at hand."

"About your motion here, you have to be focused and stay on the points you need to approach the judge. They do not process hearsay, which your text is full of. They get only facts. The more evidence and facts you submit to the court, the better chances you have that the judge will rule in your favor."

As I looked at him, I saw myself as the motion presented me, playing the role of angry and innocent victim of circumstances, realizing my initial motion was full of emotion and accusations that could be difficult or impossible to prove. I had treated it more as a tirade instead of an objective report. But how can one anticipate such a stance? How can you live your life as if it needed to be defended like this? Vince must have sensed my distress at his response, for he was patient with me while maintaining a firm message.

"You're not alone here, David. I have experienced at first hand for years the pain and suffering you're going through. But the fact that your wife is a psychologist isn't in your favor. You're starting unequally in the scale of justice," my guest said, articulating the last sentence in a near whisper, as if it was a final judgment in its own right. "The family courts work closely with psychologists, and the family judges rely on them for many major decisions. These psychologists are the experts that allow the family court to function. There is no jury here. The judge will decide with input from these specialists. Your wife, as a Doctor of Psychology, will know how to manipulate the system — with the help of her lawyer. This is reality and you have to accept it."

Vince's earnest face was suddenly transformed with his straight delivery of fact. First he smiled nervously, as though he understood how much he discouraged me with his last statement, but again that vivid sense of bitterness and pain appeared on his features. I felt certain he was revisiting memories of his own past when he had faced his foes and challenges. Then he rallied and spoke again with kindness.

"It will be difficult, David, but I'll do my best to help you through it. I have experienced worse things than what you're going through," he added calmly. But for me his statement was like the calm before the storm. There he stood, with his mighty shovel behind him, having buried the past into memory, while I was the victim whose future doom was being announced, regardless of his words of assurance. I had a sudden desire to shut him up and to swear at him, to mock him, but I knew this was unfair, a reaction that had more to do with my state of mind than his. He was sincere in presenting the truth in his own way. And though he offered me hope, he made no promises.

"You're either angry or in shock," Vince began. Then he gave me a startled look, like he'd been stung by a bee, giving me the sense he was again reliving his past experiences. With his uncertain smile he said, "So your spouse was an illegal immigrant when she met you, and she filed for divorce while being a temporary resident. Our smart lawmakers gave illegal immigrants many ways to transform themselves into legal citizens of this country. This nation needs cheap labor and these immigrants usually work for far less than others. Your wife's immigration status will give her a boost here."

"What's the connection of family court to immigration laws?" I asked, surprised that he would bring up the topic. Maya had immigration issues that involved deception she was caught at, but I didn't put the two topics together at that point. After all, my parents too were immigrants to this country. Vince knew this would take some explaining. "Let's have a drink before we continue," Vince suggested, pointing to the bottle of wine that sat beside us untouched. I realized my own problems had overwhelmed my duties as a host. I poured two glasses of a good Shiraz vintage into glasses and at his suggestion, we toasted to my success in court. It felt good to share a glass of wine with this man, someone who understood the challenges I faced far better than I did.

"Lately there have been many cases similar to yours regarding immigration and marriage rights," Vince said, sipping his wine slowly, as if savoring the drink. "Several weeks ago I heard about an immigration fraud case brought by the husband that was dismissed because the wife claimed domestic violence."

"But she was a battered wife, not an immigration criminal, wasn't she?" I asked.

"You have to think of her as a criminal in this case, because the same thing is going to happen to you," Vince said, watching my reaction.

"I never raised my hands on my spouse or my children! If I did I would be ex-communicated by my family!" I exclaimed.

Vincent looked up at some point on the ceiling as though something was written there. Was he wondering if I was going to be too dull or difficult to convince? Or was he merely startled by his prediction? But he spoke with such quiet authority, with no obvious ego displayed; I knew I must listen carefully to his advice.

"In most of these cases there is no domestic violence in play. But the moment your spouse knows that her immigration case will be denied because she didn't stay married until she got her citizenship, you will most likely become accused of domestic violence regardless of the truth. And who can prove otherwise?" He paused for a second and again smiled, watching my vaguely delirious manner, leaning on the table with one hand, eyes wandering around the room in a pained expression.

"You're now legally engaged with an untrustworthy woman. Or your wife was untrustworthy from the beginning. I suggest you take notes from now on, notes that include your daily schedule and where you are at any moment."

"Why should I do this? What purpose will it serve?" I asked, acting out a denial that was slowly melting into realization.

Vince continued in a straightforward, serious tone.

"In this country, if a woman can convince the judge she had suffered domestic violence, she doesn't need consecutive three years of married residence in order to get citizenship, neither your signature as a spouse. Your spouse has a strong motive to use the system in order to get a restraining order against you. She would likely file false police reports and accuse you of all sorts of abuse."

At this my left hand started trembling, and I leaned forward with both hands on the desk. I didn't expect this training session to be so blunt and frightening. I sensed that it was the truth that he spoke, and not mere guessing. I realized Vince was preparing me for a battle, as if he was my officer. Recalling my military days when I heard it so often, the most-used phrase: *Hard in training, easy in battle*, I knew he was preparing me for upcoming enemies with the seriousness of real war.

Vince frowned and again looked steadily at my face, perhaps wondering at my naiveté. We both knew this fight would not be easy, and the outcome totally unpredictable.

"From now forward, David, you're a lame duck in the eyes of the law enforcement. Your wife will file many false reports, and it is just a matter of time before she gets a restraining order to present to the immigration authorities."

This damning prophecy in particular, the specificity of his words, made a deep impression on me. This man was speaking from knowledge, not opinion. He was saying that the famous legal system of the Brave and the Free can be unbalanced and unfair, and far worse. I realized his words were meant to educate and shock me, to prepare me for the modern -day war of the family that many must endure. But I was still in a state of shock, facing the future.

"I cannot believe this can happen in the United States courts," I said more to myself at that point. "How can justice work like this? When has man had to endure such a terrible confrontation as this, with a woman who had been the love of my life, my very life blood?" "Women have never had so many rights in history," Vince answered, "including the right for easy divorce. I'm sure it is difficult for them also, when they realize the aftermath of these rights, especially when these are abused."

He spoke of no personal issues, uttered no names. He merely stated what he feels women experience from his point of view, and I was surprised to hear this sympathetic view, considering his horrific experiences with his ex- wife, one he didn't name, far worse than mine, he had said. But he was either a gentle man by nature, or had been worn down by his own battles to a new level of calm and acceptance. To me the situation was unthinkable, almost surreal. But I knew I had to move forward, and not waste Vince's very good and well-meant counsel. I stated, "All right then! I'll start carrying a log and record my whereabouts. Let's go over the motion. I have until Friday to file it."

Vince then raised the papers that took me weeks to prepare and started crossing out section after section. He continued to read as I watched him scratch out large portions of my printed toil as useless. Fifteen minutes later, when he was done, he said, "Remember this fact, the court isn't interested in hearsay or your opinions. They will respond only to provable issues where you can submit evidence. The legal business is very technical, with many variables that deviate from the judge's opinions and prejudices, the lawyers' appeal in the court and participation in perjury of their clients. But the bottom line is what tangible proof you have to support your position versus the opponent's position. The game is played like chess and poker combined, and you need to play it right."

He then worked with me to finalize the first motion, showing me how to organize the complicated paper- work. I made three copies — one for the court, one to be served to my spouse's lawyer and one for me.

As we finished our work and our drinks, I thanked my new friend for his assistance. As he rose to leave, I had a sense of his compassion for my predicament. But after he left for home, I fell asleep immediately as it seemed that for the first time in months, I was back in control of my destiny and my finances. Or so I told myself.

CHAPTER FIVE

The Restraining Order

I woke up on Saturday morning to the persistent sound of the phone that had lately been ringing endlessly while I slept. Just as I picked up the phone I heard a click. Why do they always call and hang up? Not even a good morning! It was nearly 9 a.m. when I finally stretched and looked out of the window. I was scheduled to fly this afternoon in my beloved Piper Cherokee.

Looking in my closet for warm clothes, I was suddenly startled by a series of strong knocks on my door. Who comes knocking so early on Saturday morning, could it be my wife on a surprise visit with our children? But that was just part of my dream, I told myself. She would do nothing of the sort to please me. It was probably my neighbor who sometimes comes to borrow something.

When I looked through the peephole on the door and saw a middle-aged woman in a uniform, strange thoughts started to flash in my head. I just couldn't guess who she was and what she wanted from me, knocking so aggressively on my door. When I opened the door and let the woman in, she identified herself as the local Sheriff, here to serve me with papers my wife had requested, a restraining order, just as Vince had predicted. I offered her a seat on one of the chairs at my dining table.

"What am I accused of now?" I said with desperation I couldn't hide. "My spouse in this divorce process just doesn't leave me alone!"

"Don't worry, mister," the Sheriff answered calmly. "I do this on a daily basis. You will have your due process in court." She then handed me the temporary restraining order papers and asked me to sign in several places.

"Your hearing is on Monday morning at the Monmouth Courthouse, nine o'clock. Be there on time. Judge Killmen starts her sessions promptly."

"From her name I can assume that she'll kill me if I do not show up!" I said, trying to get a smile from the woman.

"Be there on time and try to get a lawyer!" she answered with a straight face. No funny business.

When she left I immediately called Vince and questioned him on what I should expect on Monday at this hearing, expressing my anxiety over what lengths Maya would go to ruin me.

"Relax! There are thousands of men like you in New Jersey being served with these orders."

"That's what the Sheriff implied. But it doesn't make me feel any better."

"This is part of the divorce game, where men are usually the victims. Her moves will be predicable, as I've been saying."

I knew Vince was trying to calm me down, but I was still anxious. It was frightening to imagine what level of inhumanity my ex- love was capable of, pushing me down and rubbing me into the dirt. The lies were already starting, sooner than either of us would have guessed.

"I'll try to coach you on what to say and how to conduct yourself in this trial. As we discussed, you might succeed without representation, as many lawyers there will just take your money and do a lousy job. I do not have the stats on how many bad lawyers vs. good there are out there. There are some very good lawyers who really do care about their clients and doing what is right. But even with a good lawyer it's difficult to know what direction a judge will take even when you think you know that judge. Some people get lucky with lawyers, finding someone who works hard, is acknowledged by the judges and proceeds correctly. "

"Why did the Sheriff tell me to get a lawyer?" I asked. Did she really have my interests in mind? Who really knows how to proceed?"

"Everyone will tell you to do so," he said. "It's how the system works."

From following the media for years, I did know that trial outcomes depend heavily on the lawyers representing the defendants. Of course, I never thought that I would be on trial, or in a situation where I needed to find a good lawyer who knew what he or she was doing. And Vince may feel that since he beat the system, anyone can do it if determined and willing to do the work — an attitude I was starting to doubt. But how can one know until it is too late? Where do you get that kind of confidence when your spouse is undermining every move you make?

"Vince, Maya claimed I telephoned her, when I do not have her phone number. I was just asking Judge Irish for the rights to phone my children, as we discussed in the last motion you helped me write. In the papers she had filed against me she claimed that I had said to her "Something bad will happen if you won't give up custody." What type of cheap language is that? Why should I say something like that a week before family court hearing, when I was merely hoping to regain visitation rights, not full custody? How can I defend myself with this female judge?"

I knew I sounded desperate, and Vince was getting the picture that his success story would not necessarily translate to mine — perhaps because of my desperation? Was it acting classes I really needed for this affair? Was my own emotional state going to be held against me? After all, Vince was cool and collected by nature, while I was certainly capable of getting hot-headed and caustic when pushed.

But we were both in a state of surprise. After working together on all the motions, we didn't expect this restraining order just a week before the Family Judge decision on the issues I had filed. I was certain Maya didn't want me to ever see the children, though she certainly wanted me to continue paying child support and alimony, while living in our marital home.

"Maya will be there with her mother and sister," I explained, "and they are unscrupulous and will lie bluntly. They do it well. I think I should take the Sheriff's advice."

"Your choice, David. I've got to run, so speak with you later," Vince said before hanging up. He sounded disappointed in my decision, but he understood by then my insecurities and hesitance about not having legal help. He realized that for me a restraining order was a complete humiliation, a personal attack on my character, and of course, it was an open door for false arrests in the future.

As a law-abiding citizen, I did respect the court, the so-called orderly and fair processes managed by the police and judges that allow our system of crime and punishment to work. I never thought that I would be caught in the grinding wheels of Justice.

When I was in my last court session with Judge Irish, I caught a glimpse of Judge Killmen in court, and after seeing her, I got the impression she wasn't particularly sympathetic to men, and didn't seem to like them. So I made the decision to get a lawyer after all, largely due to the running thoughts I had about this judge, and the suggestion of the sheriff.

Now that we were getting so close to the confrontation, I didn't believe that I would have an equal chance surviving in this system of justice without a lawyer — me, being of Spanish Jewish origins, with an Irish Judge, and three European women who happen to be pathological liars? I didn't like to think this way, but I had experienced such attitudes before. All Jews have. It's part of our history. So I called one of the law firms on the internet and set an appointment with them.

On Monday morning I entered the Town of Freehold and drove to the courthouse in the maze of the interlocking and one-way streets. During the last year's frequent visits to this courthouse, I realized that unless I memorized a specific path and followed it exactly without any deviations or short cuts, it would be difficult to find that building. Now that the schools were open, I had to wait behind a row of busses, but I didn't dare deviate from my route.

When I met my lawyer, I was shocked and disappointed. He was young and likely inexperienced, definitely not the person I talked to on the phone. I felt my left arm muscle twitching, which happens only when I encounter great anxiety. There was no way out at this point, and I figured that my chances of having a decent defense had just dissipated into thin air. What bad luck! The young lawyer approached me and held out his hand.

"Mr. Tal?"

"Yes," I answered hesitantly, shaking his hand, trying to dispel my strong sense of distrust.

"Hi. I'm Todd Prone. Mr. Johansson couldn't be here as he was assigned a different court case, so I was assigned yours."

"He should have notified me of this change to my legal representation."

"He did mention to you that the firm is representing you. That means any lawyer in our firm," Todd answered abruptly with a note of sarcasm.

I was relieved when a group of people passed by and one paused to say, 'Hi Todd! How are you?' I knew at that moment that Todd was known in this courthouse. Maybe he could handle my case with some skill after all.

"Is this Judge Killmen's courtroom?" I asked Todd as he stopped before a pair of big heavy metal doors. He nodded and we walked inside. I'd heard that Judge Killmen had been assigned to handle hearings of final restraining cases for years and by that knowledge I hoped for an experienced judge.

The courtroom was a large white room, with six rows of elongated benches, a fake oak panel converted to a low fence with a gate on one side, separating the people from the podium of the Judge. Behind the fence were two sets of chairs, one for the defendant and lawyer on the right, and on the left sat the plaintiff and lawyer. The judge would sit behind the large oak table installed over a raised floor, a podium more like a miniature stage.

A court assistant standing next to the door led me to my seat in the front row, with several other gloomy-looking men. The one seated next to me was a scruffy-looking middle-aged man, who hadn't shaved for weeks. He just sat down there quietly with his lowered head held between both hands.

Two seats to my right a young man dressed with blue jeans and a T-shirt was seated clumsily. His head kept slowly turning, as though he was constantly scanning the room, and his eyes kept moving around rapidly. He presented a forced smile when we crossed looks, a smile that didn't seem natural or appropriate. He was perhaps trying to look cool, as his wife or girlfriend who had filed this restraining order against him was probably sitting somewhere in the courtroom.

First, the cases to be heard with legal representation were announced. My heart was pounding rapidly as I heard my name called and I was discouraged when it was decided to take our case first, for now I couldn't learn from others how to answer cross-examinations and get depositions. On the other hand, I could get back to my work early. For me, time was money, as I didn't get paid when not physically present in my office, albeit my time was worth much less, money wise, than the time of the lawyers surrounding me.

As I scanned the faces of the men seated next to me, I got a nervous twitch in one of the muscles of my right leg, and I assumed that it was caused by my anxiety of the situation. Violent emotional turmoil and conflicting thoughts on the legal system were consuming me as I came up with new thoughts on the impossibility of my situation.

With a sense of increasing emotional disconnection that soldiers often face before a battle, I felt that it was like the time I stood facing the open door of the C-130 Hercules troop carriers before my first training jump. Viewing the earth down below, with the tremendous noise and irrational fears, I had become numb to my fate, even though I was carrying not only one parachute, but a spare one if needed. The whole jump would only last 90 seconds. But the jump in court I was now facing was of uncertain length and outcome. And for me, its consequences could be as deadly as a free-fall without a parachute.

The female court guard opened another door of the courtroom, one with a big brass knocker and a lock above it, and in walked a tall uniformed officer with his right hand tucked behind his gun holster. The officer, with no smile in his face, looked like a stereotypical uniformed officer of the law. He had a hard jaw, his mouth tightly pressed into a mild grimace, and an athletic build, with his pants tucked into his boots. The court guard pointed toward the first row and this athletic officer approached me, pulling his shoulders straight back with a gesture of authority.

"Please come with me and walk ahead of me toward the door!" he commanded. I jumped like a puppet and started walking towards the door, glancing at the people seated in the courtroom. I could see Maya, her mother and her sister, all wearing infantile smiles of dominance. I imagined they felt good seeing me in this situation, or seeing any other man in the same situation. All three of them had a bad history with the men in their family and in their country, and this situation was the payback as I represented all men who had ever got close to them.

I felt their mocking grins drilling my back as I passed them. I knew that Maya's mother enjoyed the situation the most as she saw me taken away by the officer, and I felt that I should have empathy for her, albeit her blindness and pleasure in seeing me humiliated. The officer led me through a long narrow passage with several doorways and dim lights, like those in the dull hallways of any government building. When we entered a tiny room at the end of the corridor, I drew my breath and stood listening, waiting for instructions.

There was no sound for several seconds as the officer put on his disposable nylon gloves. Suddenly, he turned to me and broke his silence, while I listened anxiously. "Please turn your back to me. I'm going to conduct a body search for any possible weapon you may have concealed on your body."

"I don't have any weapons! Why are you doing this?" How could I remain cool after having to start the procedure like a convicted criminal?

"It's the law and regulations in this courthouse," the officer answered in an understanding tone.

"I was once an Air Force officer and I never thought I would be in such a situation unless taken prisoner of war," I said, as if talking to a sympathetic ear. Certainly he respected the Air Force. He probably recognized the humiliation many law-abiding men feel when they have to go through this process. Maybe he actually empathized with the men he examined every day. After all, he was just doing his job. His face was less threatening than when I first saw him, making me feel more at ease.

Then my concept of humanity seen through his eyes popped like a flash before me. This is his daily chore. He sees dozens like me on a daily basis, including the hard criminals, and probably he doesn't feel compassion for anyone at this point. He's just putting on a good cop act. This though struck with lightning reality, and it was harsh. I was glad to face what might be the truth. After all, I had learned much from helping Maya with her psychology classes, where one had to try to find how the human mind really works, instead of living in a fantasy world built by dreamers and romantics.

The officer turned towards me and again with a stern look of authority said, "Let's returns to the courtroom. You're done."

"Thank you, officer," I replied, following him through the passage that resembled a hospital corridor. While walking, I about what this man saw every day and suddenly, without remembering for a moment where I was going or what had happened, I found myself standing next to the door of Judge Killmen's court. I turned the metal doorknob with a tight grasp and opened the door wide.

Back in the courtroom I stood for a second observing the crowd. Over the buzz of voices, undercurrents of emotions and drama covered the room like a veil, making clarity difficult. As I walked back to the defendants' row of seats, all eyes seemed to turn toward me and the officer walking behind me. I noticed the giggling and smirks emanating from my spouse, her mother and her sister.

As the security checks continued quietly, with the officers leading each one of the defendants to the examining room and back, I could understand why it was necessary. This room was packed with the most intense emotions, and some men or women as a matter of fact could easily crack under the heavy circumstances, propagated with lies told by family members, or decisions made by a presiding judge. If there was a weapon available somewhere in the room, I could certainly see someone using it.

Once I was back in my chair, I tried to collect my thoughts and organize them into some form of coherent order. But I couldn't do it. Any peace of mind or calming thoughts escaped me. I knew I needed to have a firm grasp of the situation, and in spite of the intense feeling of humiliation of being in this court, I was hoping to maintain an open mind, and my innocence.

My lawyer sitting next to me said, "The judge is reviewing your case now before she enters the courtroom."

"I hope she does a thorough job," I answered quietly. I hoped the judge was reviewing all the fake allegations my spouse had submitted to the court. Then doubts seeped in and I wondered how she would know that the police reports didn't hold even one bit of factual evidence. *What if she doesn't read the Youth and Family Services reports?* I was praying that the judge would not be biased. *She certainly wouldn't decide on her verdict even before coming out of her chambers, would she? After all, this is the divine process of the law,* I told myself, *the human evolutionary proceedings given to us by God and delivered to mankind by Moses.* I respected that.

"All rise!" The court guard suddenly announced with his loud and screechy voice.

The crowd in the room suddenly stood up in silence and all eyes were directed to a single point, a small wooden door set in the courtroom back wall. Judge Killmen entered the courtroom through this door and approached her bench behind the heavy oak table. She was in her late fifties, with blond thick hair collected carelessly into a bun at the back of her head. She was dressed in a worn robe and scuffed shoes, and her stern expression made her look authoritative, dull-witted and rude in her position of established authority.

"Please be seated!" the judge yelled in a voice that sounded like a commanding scream.

"The first case to be heard is Tal versus Tal!" The court guard announced loudly.

The court guard led Maya to her seat and then led me and my lawyer to our seats facing the large table. Watching my wife, I noticed she was heavier than the last time I'd seen her. Her posture was tense; her hair didn't have its usual reddish tint, and was dyed a dull blonde. She wore a finely tailored blue suit, a plain white blouse and pearl earrings I had never seen — probably a gift from her lover. Maya was always good at getting her man to give her gifts and I knew her shopping habits, too. Every bill from our joint past showed up on my credit card statement, which I paid quietly never daring to raise objections, as I had learned the consequences of objecting to her spending.

Suddenly Maya's green eyes turned towards me as though she was compelled to do so. Her stare was empty, with an underlying intense anger. *This woman is filled with hatred and her heart is empty,* I thought to myself looking back to the judge. *Yes, she's filled with lies that were building in layers, with no room for remembering how I had taken care of her for so many years.* I thought with a shudder, "

Oh, God, please help me! What situation have you put me through after 11 years of dedication to my family? How did I end up in this courtroom?

I thought of the trial of Colonel Alfred Dreyfus which had occurred about hundred and twenty years back, wrongfully accused by the government and finally pardoned after the writer Émile Zola shamed them with his famous "J'accuse" essay.

Now I hoped for a modern day Emile Zola — a man who had risked his career and even his life to speak the truth about government injustice — to be here for me and in my case, and speak out against my spouse's false accusations. But when I looked at my young lawyer, I knew he was no Emile Zola, and my problems were not uncommon. Many had traveled down this path with little or no help from a competent advocate, I reminded myself. As Vince and that woman Sheriff had said, "I'm not alone, though why do I feel so isolated?"

CHAPTER SIX

The Trial

The trial that could turn me into a criminal and award me a record had begun. And Judge Killmen seemed ready to kill this man as she organized her papers and glanced at me with a down-turned mouth and crooked frown.

JUDGE KILLMEN: Maya Tal versus David Tal. The docket number is FV-130-817-09. First, may I have the appearance of counsel for the defendant?

TODD PRONE: Your Honor, Todd Prone from the law offices of John F. Thorne on behalf of David, who's present in court to my right.

JUDGE: "Good morning, Todd Prone."

TODD: "Good morning, Your Honor."

JUDGE: "Would both parties please stand? Place your left hands on the Bible, and raise your right hands. My court clerk will administer the oath to you."

TODD: "Your Honor, would it be okay if my client affirmed?"

JUDGE: "Yes, he can affirm, absolutely; just raise your right hand."

After my wife, the plaintiff, was sworn in, and I gave my affirmation, the judge now knew I wasn't Christian. Assuming she was an Irish Catholic, I wondered if my lawyer chose the right move here, making our religious differences evident. My mind wasn't clear and I started assuming that the judge might be biased. However, I have met many biased people and somehow to deduce from the masses to the private individual, the Judge sitting in front of me, wasn't appropriate, but the thought still crossed my mind. *The Bible is such a powerful icon; would a man who refuses to swear by it be looked at with disfavor by a Catholic?*

I couldn't stop worrying about every little detail that might put me at a disadvantage, as minor as they might seem. But another thing I knew from my second-hand studies of psychology — people make decisions based on instincts and emotions far more often than they would like to admit. Reason and logic were goals to aspire to, as if a fine theory that was still not thoroughly tested, instead of foundations of behavior.

Seeing Maya sitting there, I thought of when I had first met her, the woman who had brought me to this trial. How she had changed since then inside as well as out. Had I, too, become a new person? Someone neither of us imagined would become in this marriage? And there we stood, side by side, stating our name that had no meaning to my wife, not anymore. The questions and answers started.

COURT CLERK: "Please say your name, spell your last name."
MAYA: " Maya, T-A-L."
DAVID: "David, T-A-L."
JUDGE: "Thank you, please be seated."
TODD: "Your Honor, as a preliminary matter, I know that there are a few witnesses involved in this case as well. I would just request that they sit outside the courtroom during the testimony of Maya."
JUDGE: "Let me just ask some preliminary questions and then I'll do that."
TODD: "Okay, thank you."
JUDGE: "Maya, you're ready to proceed today?"
MAYA: "Yes."
JUDGE: "I'm going to ask you some questions about what it is that occurred and what it is that might have occurred in the past. And then Todd Prone will have the ability to ask you questions on cross examination. And then if you feel that there's something else you want me to

know, I'll listen to that. After your testimony is done, I'll hear any witnesses who are called on your behalf. Do you have any witnesses?"

MAYA: "Yes, I do."

JUDGE: "How many witnesses?"

MAYA: "Two."

JUDGE: "And who are they?"

MAYA: "My mom and my sister. "

JUDGE: "Okay. Now, was I told that one of your witnesses requires the assistance of an interpreter?"

MAYA: "Yes, that's correct."

JUDGE: "And the interpreter is here?"

MAYA: "Yes."

JUDGE: "Okay. So who needs the interpreter?"

MAYA: "My mom."

JUDGE: "We will hear her and then your sister. And likewise, Todd Prone will have the ability to ask them questions in cross-examination. After your case is complete, Todd Prone will ask questions of his client with regard to the issues. And Todd Prone, do you have any witnesses to call?"

TODD: "No, Your Honor. Just David."

JUDGE: "So after I hear from the defendant, after you've asked questions, and Todd Prone has asked questions, I'll make my decision, okay? So I would ask that the witnesses step out into the hall and we'll call them in one by one. All right, Maya. What's your relationship to the defendant?"

MAYA: "We're in divorce proceedings. He's legally still my husband but we do not reside together."

JUDGE: "So there's a current divorce proceeding?"

MAYA: "Yes."

JUDGE: "And are you represented by an attorney in that divorce?"

MAYA: "Not any longer. I was. "

JUDGE: "Okay. And how long has the divorce been going on? "

MAYA: "Since December 14th last year, about 12 months ago."

JUDGE: "And do you have an order regarding custody, parenting time and support?"
MAYA: "Yes."
JUDGE: "And so the two of you were living separate and apart from one another?"
MAYA: "Yes."
JUDGE: "And when did you separate?"
MAYA: "Back in January."
JUDGE: "And did you remain in what was the marital home or did you —?"
MAYA: "Yes, I'm in the house. David moved out. "

Actually, I was forced to move out. I had no choice. I won't forget that moment, with only my suitcase quickly packed, closing the front door behind me as my young daughter watched from the living room window, holding her favorite teddy bear my parents had given her. I had to leave the house I had carefully chosen for a family, a home to be proud of.

I kept silent and let my lawyer continue. Facts are facts. I knew I wasn't supposed to speak spontaneously, no matter what was being said — a very difficult task for me. I had noticed how Judge Killmen was directing this show with such a careful and gentle attitude towards Maya, as if she was truly the victim who needed soothing here, not me.

From time to time when the judge glanced at me to inspect my reactions, I was shaken by her look, and my body just froze. The judge continued her questioning of Maya, taking pauses between each question.

JUDGE: "Now, is that residence currently for sale?"
MAYA: "No, not yet."
JUDGE: "Okay. And you're there with your children?"
MAYA: "Yes."
JUDGE: "And you have two children?"
MAYA: "Two children."
JUDGE: "How old are the children?"

MAYA: "Ally is eleven and Anika is five."

JUDGE: "Okay. So something happened on November the 4th that caused you to come to this court on November the 6th and get a restraining order."

MAYA: "Yes."

TODD: "Judge? I think actually it was the 3rd. And I have to object here. She wasn't actually even a party to the incident that happened on the 4th. So her testimony is on a hearsay basis. "

JUDGE: "The two people who were there at this incident are here and will be testifying. So I'll allow Maya to testify and then again, when the witnesses are sequestered."

TODD: "Okay."

I started to move in my chair, though I could find no comfortable pose. The whole process seemed so alien and false. Maya didn't receive the alleged phone call, the main subject matter of this hearing. Maya's mother and sister are foreign nationals and never have had personal relationships with me except when visiting Maya. They practically ignored me for years, except when they needed something. They currently reside in my house, enjoying the free fruits of my labor. That's the only relationship these so-called victims have with me.

JUDGE: "All right, Maya. So what happened on November the 4th, which would have been Tuesday?"

MAYA: "I think actually it was on the 3rd because the police report is from the 3rd. So I think the 4th was a mistake. On Monday I received a frantic phone call at work from my daughter and my sister. David had called up the marital residence, which he's not supposed to do because we have a civil restraint agreement. When my sister picked up the downstairs' phone, he threatened to kill her. My kids were at home that day. There was no school. My daughter usually picks up the phone, you know, before anybody else does. She was on the upstairs line so she heard that. She started yelling at him saying" How can you say something like that?" And he said "Tell your mother that something bad is going to happen to her." So my sister called the police, and Family Services got involved. They called me at work and I came home. We went to the police department. They filed an incident report. I had a DYFS worker coming to interview the kids, me and everybody else in the family."

I just sighed, and the Judge gave me a warning look. *How many lies can she tell in a few short minutes?* My mind was overworked and I became increasingly defensive, anticipating the rest of Maya's show. She now changed the story of the complaint to a threat that I was going to kill her sister. *Why would I try to kill her sister?* But would this judge see reality and the inaccurate testimony?

I started squirming in my chair, raising my head upwards, staring at different points on the ceiling with body gestures and expressions of disbelief. Judge Killmen again gave me another warning look and I instantly ceased moving. The sensation that this hearing wasn't going to be fair was becoming overwhelming. I felt it all over my body, and my stomach started to hurt, with that full pain that had been bothering me lately. How far we had come to arrive here to this place of no hope?

JUDGE: "The police called the Division of Youth and Family Services, DYFS?"
MAYA: "I believe so, yes."
JUDGE: "And DYFS interviewed the children?"
MAYA: "Yes."
JUDGE: "Did DYFS take any further action?"
MAYA: "I don't know yet. They didn't –"
JUDGE: "They're still investigating?"
MAYA: "I believe so."
JUDGE: "Now, did the police offer to file a temporary restraining order for you?"
MAYA: "They did. They sent me to Freehold to file it."
JUDGE: "Okay. And did you file the temporary restraining order?"
MAYA: "I did."
JUDGE: "So if the incident happened on the 3rd, how come you

went to file the complaint on the 6th?"

MAYA: "Because I was working nights. I couldn't get off work to do it. I sometimes work double shift and I can't, you know, find replacement immediately. I work in the emergency room."

JUDGE: "What towns do you live in that they referred you to Freehold?"

MAYA: "I live in Marlboro."

JUDGE: "And the Marlboro police wouldn't issue a restraining order that day?"

MAYA: "Marlboro police had been dealing with us for the entire year and because we had a civil restraint agreement, you know, we just tried to work things out. But the police have been to my house in the last year I think about forty times. Either they would be in my house, or I would be in the police station. They kept advising me to get a restraining order. And I said well, you know, I'll wait. I'll wait. Because I hope he's going to calm down. It has been a year since I filed for divorce. But instead of calming down, things just keep on happening."

I was aghast at this performance. If there had been a death threat, Maya would have filed the temporary restraining order immediately, and the police would have been involved right away. The police just sent her away and Maya took her time to file the order, as she had other priorities. The judge should know that a death threat is a serious issue, but Maya waited three days to report it. If I was a real threat, her sister could have been dead by that time. And there was Maya, bold enough to continue this falsity right in the face of Judge Killmen. I watched their exchange with growing dread.

JUDGE: "So, who was your attorney when you got the civil restraining order?"

MAYA: "It was Mr. Newberg. I changed lawyers later. With Mr. Newberg's advice, we agreed on civil restraints, things we dealt with before. So Mr. Newberg said, you know, you're in a divorce proceeding. Let's calm things down. Let's sign this agreement and David is going to hold to it. But civil restraint agreements do not have any standing within the police department or anywhere else and so David continued harassing us. He calls my work constantly. He threatens people. He asks for my schedule. Any place I go, I go to my dentist, in Freehold, they notified me that my husband called."

TODD: "Objection."

JUDGE: "It doesn't go to the truth of the matter asserted. It's not that he actually called. It's just a matter of what she's being told. So I'll not sustain that objection."

JUDGE: "How often would you say he calls you at work?"

MAYA: "He calls my work weekly. At least once a week. I'm not always there at work, but he calls even if I'm not there."

JUDGE: "And you say he has followed you?"

MAYA: "He does follow me, yes."

JUDGE: "When was the last time you saw him following you?"

MAYA: "The last time was I believe — "

JUDGE: "Take your time."

MAYA: "I think it was in October."

JUDGE: "And do you remember the circumstances of him following you?"

MAYA: "Yes, I do. We went for economic mediation with Mr. Serabin and I think it's in Ocean County, a town in Ocean County. And after the mediation, David followed me on the Parkway. He cut me off on Route 9 where it connects with 516 West."

JUDGE: "And when was that?"

MAYA: "That was in July — July 14th. I immediately called pound 77 to report that he cut me off. I had to slam my brakes to avoid hitting his car. They said they were going to contact Marlboro police and advised me to stop by the Marlboro police station. I went there and filed a report. They told me the next time someone follows you, you're supposed to call 911 immediately, not pound 77. I didn't know these things, but they filed the report anyway."

JUDGE: "Okay. It says here that he has accessed your personal records?"

MAYA: "He did access them. The way I found out was through Judge Irish's papers. David filed a motion about financial stuff and it's going to be heard on the 5th. He attached the records from my computer to this motion. It turns out he also knows exactly what I'm doing with my sister's travel plans, the exact amount of money she pays for, whatever it is. I don't know how he accesses this information because we don't have anything together. We live completely apart. He has his own stuff, I have my own. And I have no idea how it's even possible to do this."

The clouds of lies surrounding these imaginary stories were so dense that I had a hard time wading through it. *How could I get information from her computer when I wasn't living there?* I'd have to be a pretty good hacker to do that. She forgot to mention that she went out of her way to read my manuscript on my computer. That was private, between me and my therapist.

Judge Killmen was definitely favoring Maya and directing her, not even questioning her on facts that all people in the justice system know, such as, how could I possibly call her at work when she works in a jail where all telephones are recorded and monitored? Where was the proof of this call? I again doubted the whole legal system, though I felt that it wasn't right to give up on the truth of my story being revealed in court.

Here in family court, where there was no prosecutor or jury, Maya might as well be the prosecutor, with the skills of a psychologist. She knew how to act and how to manipulate people, and the judge just let her steam ahead.

Suddenly I felt intense stomach spasms and pain radiating all over my body, I looked at Todd, thinking of asking him for a break, but I just sat here and the pain suddenly ceased.

JUDGE: "Now, you sought a restraining order in January of this year."
MAYA: "Yes."
JUDGE: "Where you say that he was waiting outside of your work and followed you."
MAYA: "That's right, he was. He continues doing that."

JUDGE: "It says here that he was tracking your car."

MAYA: "He was. Actually, the Marlboro police, Sgt. Foxman and Det. Yenisey, told me that my husband hired a private investigator to follow me."

Again, the judge allows hearsay in this trial and lets Maya lie blatantly. No Marlboro police officers were in attendance. If they had been no one would make such a ridiculous statement, but the Judge still accepted it as the whole truth.

JUDGE: "And he was waiting outside your work on January 15th?"

MAYA: " He was waiting outside my work, yes. I walked out with my coworkers. They actually saw his car there."

JUDGE: "Have you seen him outside your work since then?"

MAYA: "I haven't seen him at my work, at prison, because there are cameras all around which he avoids. But I have seen him at Holy Trinity Hospital."

JUDGE: "And when was the last time you think you saw him?"

MAYA: "About a month ago."

JUDGE: "You also work at the hospital?"

MAYA: "Yes, I work in two places. For my day job, I'm a psychologist for the State of New Jersey. I work for a sex -offender treatment program in a prison. And I work in the emergency room at Holy Trinity Hospital."

JUDGE: "Now, in January, it says that you filed a restraining order based upon the fact that apparently he handed you a manuscript he was writing."

MAYA: "Yes."

JUDGE: "And in the last chapter it described how he was going to fly a plane into your house in Marlboro?"

MAYA: "Yes."

JUDGE: "Is he a writer?"

MAYA: "Not that I know of. He's supposed to be a computer programmer. I think he has recently taken up writing."

Maya, after complaining that I was hacking her computer, was accessing my therapy sessions? Judge Killmen knew the document was used in therapy and yet didn't say anything about the illegality of using it in court. Meanwhile, my lawyer was just standing there, making no effort to stop this onslaught of lies. He'd already been paid, so I guess he didn't care.

No one was truly helping me here. Not Emile Zola, nor my lawyer, and not God. While I had always believed that the courts and our legal system were there at God's will, to instill law and order in humanity and distinguish us from the wild, I would soon learn otherwise.

Still, I tried to hold onto some hope for justice. *I must not make conclusions based on this one event,* I told myself. Accurate deductions can only be based on events pointing to the same conclusions. But though I tried to think this way, the tide was definitely turning against me.

I had a heavy feeling in the pit of my stomach that ate away at my hopes as Judge Killmen continued her questioning of Maya. Suddenly I felt intense stomach spasms and pain again. I looked at Todd and then I asked the Judge for a break of several minutes. I was escorted out while the Judge announced a five minute break and then entered her chambers turning her head towards me. As she entered through her door, dismay was written all over her face.

CHAPTER SEVEN

Meeting Maya

I went to the Court's cafeteria area escorted by a court officer, and grabbed a seat. I still felt some pain in my stomach but I felt much better out of the courtroom. I sat down and my memories suddenly flashed to the early days 11 years ago, when I had met Maya, the woman who had brought me to this trial.

Summer had ended and with it all the outdoor singles' activities and the singles' bar scenes of New York City. Fall had started and the days became shorter and my way home to Long Island on my daily commute seemed almost endless, just to reach home for some late evening TV viewing and a good night's sleep alone. One day while sitting and reading the single's section in one of the New York newspapers, an advertisement caught my eye. I found a new venue on how to be introduced to women through a matchmaker dating service. This matchmaker dating service offered introductions to Eastern European women. I'd met some Russian girls in the past, which added to the stereotype-building mechanism every person innately feels. Yes, they were generally good-looking and that stereotype built an internal, unexplained urge to go and visit that dating agency.

On one cold and foggy night in November, I was set up on a blind date. I thought this date would be a casual thing with no future. I went to meet my date hesitantly, driving my smashing Rolls-Royce, just to make a first good impression. I only used this car for special occasions — in the last six years I'd only added 6,000 miles to its odometer.

I loved this car. It had a shiny teak dashboard and leather seats that looked and smelled posh and high class. I used to polish the car once a month and the smell of the polish always seeped in while I was driving. I could never thoroughly understand men's fascination with cars, until I owned this one. I saw it as an entry for me into the world of moneyed people. It was my fantasy car.

I arrived at the Queens, New York, address given to me by the dating agency got out of my car. A cold wind was blowing and the bare trees rattled with every gust. From where I was standing, I could see a young girl timidly looking at me. She was standing next to the entrance of the building listed on my address sheet. She started walking toward me, and I just stared at her with curiosity and admiration.

Though I was looking at her for the first time, I felt I had known her for ages. She brightened my heart immediately and I knew she was the one. I didn't know anything about her living conditions, her immigration status or her marriage separation issues then; I'd learn all of that later.

"David?" she asked with a thick Eastern European accent. Her tone was soft and her accent wasn't Russian.

"Hi, Maya. Nice to meet you," I answered , my voice trembling slightly. I opened the door of the car and invited her inside. She stared for a second at the car's interior like she didn't recognize the make of the car. She later mentioned that she thought the car was a Lincoln town.

Maya wasn't the prettiest of the girls I'd met in the last few months, but she was attractive. She also wasn't the friendliest, but for some reason I still felt she was an angel sent from above — a gift from heaven. I started imagining her with wings and a crown. She had something I hadn't found in other women I'd met. It was something I couldn't understand and somehow made me desperately seek her love and company. From that day forward, I'd treat her like an angel sent from God in a human form.

We started on our way and drove ahead to New York City. Maya was relatively quiet and needed encouragement to discuss any topic I brought up.

Her thick accented slow responses endeared her to me even more. I felt the charges of passion building within me. The more I looked at her, the more I felt it.

We arrived at New York City, the Big Apple, and I parked my car at a lot next to My Fair Lady restaurant. The waiter seated us next to the window at my request and lit the large candle in the center of our table.

Maya was staring around the well decorated restaurant, and it seemed she was feeling slightly uncomfortable. I wasn't sure that I had brought her to the right place since Maya wasn't really dressed appropriately for this restaurant, but I didn't care. Women are never required to follow a dress code in fancy restaurants, so she was fine.

Maya wasn't aware of my gaze, and in that moment I noticed something in her eyes that troubled me. I got the impression that she was used to fancy restaurants like this. I was hoped that Maya would notice me and study me as any woman would do on a first date, but she was busy looking around the restaurant.

The head waiter approached us and offered us menus while rattling off the specials of the day. I told the waiter that we needed time to look at the menu and would call him when we were ready. I felt that Maya was embarrassed because she wasn't familiar with what was offered on the menu and was silently asking me to choose for her. I was elated by when I received her approval for sending the waiter away.

On our next date, I decided to take Maya for a flying lesson. I'd only done this with one other date in the past. I realized that this event meant I felt differently about Maya and our relationship. I picked her up and drove directly to Farmingdale Airport. It was a Tuesday evening and the roads were clear of the snow that had fallen a week earlier.

On the drive to the airport, Maya told me about her immigration and marital status. I knew I liked her and was determined to do everything for her. Her issues would not be a problem for me —I regarded myself as a problem solver.

After a short flying lesson, I drove Maya to my house. She was speechless when we approached the big house with the lit swimming pool behind it. I was well off, though certainly not rich, but hoped she was impressed by my home.

She was a young immigrant without many financial resources, so she definitely was impressed. I did my best to make myself appear appealing to her in all ways.

Maya was young and good-looking girl. She was slim and tall and had piercing green eyes. Her mother was Latvian and her father was Ukrainian and she had moved here from Latvia. She said she was "mixed up" about her identity and ethnicity because she came from a "mixed" background.

In school she grew up between the cultures and experienced the clash and differences between the people in Latvia. Her step-dad was Latvian, and considered himself a pure ethnic Latvian who always pursued independence from the Russians and their forced settlement in Latvia. He regarded Maya and her sister as half breeds and hardly communicated with them.

Maya's birth father was Ukrainian and a retired pilot. Through her early childhood he was close to his children. When Maya was 12 years old, her parents decided to divorce. The divorce was difficult. Maya's father moved back to his home country of Ukraine, and never saw his children again.

The divorce impacted Maya for the rest of her life. She wrote the following letter that summarizes her feelings about her parents' divorce, just before her graduation from her PhD in psychology 10 years later.

Maya's Letter

*My parents' divorce was a very unpleasant and heartbreaking experience for all of us. At the time when my father decided to leave, my parents had been married seventeen years. I never knew that people could **have** so much hatred for each other and could so easily forget all those years that they spent together. My father left and for a number of years didn't really care how we lived. He somehow forgot that he had children. He didn't keep in touch with us and didn't pay any child support. As much as I tried, I couldn't understand what happened. All that I always knew was destroyed and shattered. My father whom I had considered a gentlemen and who was my role model suddenly changed and turned into a different person. What bothered me wasn't even the fact that he left, but that he totally forgot about us. There were no visits, no phone calls, no letters or postcards. My parents divorced in 1988 and until recently I didn't have any contact with my father.*

However, as much as I was angry with my father, I also more than anything wished to have contact with him. Somehow, the fact that he was no longer a part of my life bothered me and after many years of being angry and disappointed, I wrote a letter to my father and now I frequently keep in touch with him.

Maya was smart and cheerful and somehow hid from memory her childhood experiences, which I would later learn. Maya married a Russian man when she was 17 because her mother wanted her out of the house due to economic constraints.

This man seemed to be a loving husband but had limited intellectual and personal abilities. He used to drink and was also a womanizer. In his young adult years, he was a Russian soldier in Afghanistan and saw battle. Since then, he had emotional wounds from the battles he experienced there. Perhaps some of these hidden emotional scars reflected in the relationship with Maya, as he almost never talked about that time in his life. He once told Maya that he was happy to be out of there and he had lost many friends while being a soldier in that region.

Maya and her husband decided to move to the US after the collapse of the Soviet Union. After arriving at New York, Maya worked in a supermarket in Queens as an assistant bookkeeper and was liked by her coworkers and her manager.

Maya also had a terrifying secret, which her friends and her coworkers didn't know. She had signed for a voluntary departure in order to be able to stay and work in the US. The voluntary departure was good for one year. If she didn't leave within this fixed time frame, she would be deported.

Maya didn't see any future with her husband and lived separately from him in the same house. The only hope she had was that one day she would be lucky, and a wealthy prince would uplift her from her situation. She used to watch the movie "Pretty Woman" with Richard Gere and hoped that maybe someday she would also be lucky and meet a wealthy good-looking prince.

CHAPTER EIGHT

Early Days

Sitting in the court's cafeteria I again shifted my memories back to the time when Maya joined me at my house. The early days eleven years ago, when I had asked Maya to move in with me, the woman who had brought this trial down on my head, like a sledgehammer.

Maya and I had a beautiful beginning and I felt God had answered my prayers. I was happy to get up in the mornings and conduct my daily long commute to NYC. One month after meeting Maya, I asked her to move in with me, which she gladly did. For Maya, I was a rich man and her mother and sister were happy with her decision to move in with me.

I drove to her apartment and helped Maya move her belongings. While I was there, to my surprise I met her husband, from whom she was separated. I had a short conversation with him and he seemed quite nervous. I thought that since they were separated her husband might be at ease with her decision to move out. I was wrong.

I didn't understand until today the ease with which Maya moved away from her ex-husband after five years of marriage. I tried to find out if he was abusive to her and it turned out he wasn't. She later said that they had agreed on this separation and marrying other spouses because they didn't want to live together and it was the only way for them to stay in the United States.

It was the week before Christmas, and Maya had already been living with me for six weeks. New York City was getting ready for this holiday with many lights, decorations and sales. My cousin Martin from England had asked to spend the holiday with me and we made plans to enjoy the city together for a couple weeks. I had visited him several times before, and so it was time he visited me.

I picked Martin up at JFK Airport on a Friday evening and we drove to my house in Dix Hills, Long Island, on New York's eastern tip. It was snowing lightly, and everything was covered with snow, making the journey back home a beautiful drive through the white trees planted along the local roads. The big manicured houses of my neighborhood looked like they'd been frosted and their holiday lights painted the night with rainbow colors.

When we arrived, I could tell Martin was surprised by the large circular driveway and beautiful front yard of my home. A little drama immediately played out even before we could get out of the car. Along with the barking of my dog, came the sounds of my mother's cousin Joan yelling, "She's the devil! She's the devil!"

Joan's voice got louder as she walked briskly towards the front of the house with both fists clenched. Joan looked angry as she shouted the words again and again, like a mantra, ignoring us altogether. Once a respected professor of Native American history, Joan was now suffering from what psychologists might define as the aftermath of mini-strokes or maybe a "manageable" form of dementia.

However, the diagnosis wasn't final or clear-cut as Joan's cat-scan revealed signs of a history of multiple minor strokes. She had suffered for years from high blood pressure and diabetes and never took care of herself. She believed in self-care and herbal medicines and seemed to get along very well by herself. She was a short, good looking woman, dressed shabbily, with her hair hanging uncombed and unwashed.

As I got out of the car and came close to her, she smiled a bit awkwardly, seeing a stranger approaching behind me.

"Hi, Joan. How are you feeling?" I asked.

Martin said hello to her as well and we all stood near the porch.

"I'm fine," Joan replied shortly. "How are you, Martin?" she asked.

"Fine," he answered.

"Who is the devil?" Martin couldn't help but ask.

"David's new girlfriend!" she said, looking at me with alarm, while Martin seemed a bit startled to hear her response.

"Why is she the devil?" I asked Joan with a laugh.

"She's one of the devil's agents!" Joan replied. "I know this, for a fact!"

"Why would you say such a thing about my new girlfriend?" I asked in surprise.

"Because I'm here to protect you from her," she said in a matter-of-fact tone.

"I appreciate your concern, but I do not need protection," I answered, almost angrily. I reminded myself the woman was somewhat "off" and let it go. Little did I know then how much I would need a guardian angel in the future.

Joan was a bit obsessed with devils and angels, and she was often the best audience for my talks on one of my favorite subjects, God and creation. She also shared my fascination with cosmology and the inner workings of nature, though when she went to college, women were not encouraged to study science.

As Martin and I turned to enter my house, she stood on the front steps for a moment before following us in. Maya, the new girlfriend Joan had maligned, greeted Martin with a weak handshake. Her hand must've been cold, they usually were, and she certainly seemed to be cold towards him,too.

At the same time, Joan was sneaking up behind Martin while staring at the floor. She looked terrified, as if she saw a ghost. She then ran upstairs, ignoring Maya.

"She has her issues," I explained to Martin.

"She seems worse than when I saw a few years ago," Martin said with a nod.

Maya added with a very thick accent that sounded more like broken English, "Joan is quite sick,"

I figured Martin could barely understand what she said, so I repeated, "Joan is certainly quite sick these days," as if agreeing with Maya's more serious assessment of Joan's illness.

When we moved into the living room, Maya seemed to warm up to Martin as she continued on the subject of Joan. As she cleared the coffee table, she asked him, "What happened to her?"

He related some of Joan's history, how she used to be very pretty and was also very bright. She'd married and moved to Canada with her husband, but things didn't work out. She also had difficulties getting her PhD in history, and suffered from high blood pressure. She hadn't been the same after suffering several small strokes. "It can happen to anyone," he added.

Maya was staring at Martin with no visible expression on her face. It was apparent that she was appalled by Joan's presence in the house, even though she knew Joan was visiting. Perhaps the visit had gone on longer than she'd expected. Or maybe she was annoyed that another woman was around competing for my attention.

It seemed that Maya didn't really care what Martin was saying and she quietly walked to our bedroom. Martin didn't mention this strange behavior, and we decided to call it a night.

CHAPTER NINE

Early Married Life

I was still sitting in the court's cafeteria when the court guard asked me if I was ready to return. "Please give me several minutes more and I promise you I'll be better and ready." The guard nodded his head in agreement and went to sit across from me. I again shifted my memories back to the early times when Maya joined me at my house.

In mid- May, six months after meeting Maya, we got married. I already had noticed some relationship problems with Maya but I agreed to get married because Maya was already five months pregnant. Maya said that if we would not get married I would never see my child again. I didn't want the mother of my child to be deported and neither did I want my child to grow-up without a father.

Maya turned out to be not as submissive and agreeable as she was in the beginning of the relationship. She had a bad temper and extreme mood swings. There were many episodes of unexpected rages that started not long after Maya moved in with me. In particular, I remember a party after which she had accused me of being jealous, this though I spent most of the day at work, out of the house, not questioning or knowing what she was doing. I didn't understand the source of her accusation, or any incident that could have triggered her outburst, but I didn't respond.

I was initially shocked by her change of behavior and her outbursts, but her outbursts didn't last long as she quickly calmed down and sometimes rewarded me with a small gesture of a passionate kiss or a hug. This pattern was repeated throughout our marriage with Maya's feats of uncontrolled rage and anger always followed by sudden gestures of reconciliation without many words spoken.

After our first daughter was born, Maya seemed calmer and content and for a while she showed tenderness with the baby and with her relationship with me. In the early days of our marriage Maya had apparently been happy and she used to call me daily in order to converse with me and hear my voice.

The time after the delivery of my first-born girl was a time of elation, promise and simple bliss of married life. The night crying of our baby was part of this elated feeling of being a family man, and the long commute to work was now with purpose.

I gave Maya freedom of using her credit cards — she had acquired several — and I never questioned her purchases or spending. One late night in cold wintry November, I returned to my home after a long bus commute from NYC. The icy breeze on my face reddened my nose and ears while I walked briskly to the parking lot. I longed to be home as soon as possible, so I could see my family.

I drove home from the bus's commuter parking lot as fast as the traffic permitted. I opened the garage door and parked the car, but instead of rushing inside I decided to check the mail since I presumed the weather had prevented Maya from going to the box to get it.

There was indeed mail in the box, so I grabbed it and then went in the house. Maya was silent and didn't respond to my homecoming call so I walked up to the bedroom and found her sleeping on the bed. When I walked towards her, Maya jumped up, startled. Her eyes were wide open and she wore an expression of surprise and displeasure on her face.

"You came home early!" she exclaimed.

"Go back to sleep. I'll catch up with you later," I replied and headed towards the door.

"I'll be down in a few minutes," I heard Maya faintly respond.

"Aren't you tired, my love?" I asked.

"I was just lying down for a bit because the baby was up most of the day," she answered. She looked me up and down and asked, "Is it cold outside?"

"Yes, it is," I said and I knew that Maya hadn't stepped outside once during the day.

"Just lie down and rest. I'll be back up later," I told her gently.

I walked down to the kitchen and started opening the mail. I was surprised to see some of the credit card statements — they were even higher than the previous month. Last month, the bills were also much higher than what I had expected, but I paid with little objection. Maya liked to shop and I paid quietly in order to stay happily married.

To Maya's credit, she usually bought items in a smart way, such as sale items or reduced priced items. She purchased many items for our family's consumption, but she also bought many things that were never used and were later given away.

I was beginning to be convinced that Maya was slightly "shop-aholic," but still on the controlled side. It seemed that shopping relaxed her, but she didn't go too overboard. For me, Maya's shopping habits were typical of any woman and I never questioned her about what she had purchased and why the items she purchased were needed. Tonight, I felt differently. The bills were extremely high, which made me uneasy since in New York City there was a definite feeling that an economic slowdown was in the near future.

I heard Maya coming down the stairs and I quickly moved the bills to the side of the table.

"Hi, Maya, I hope you've rested a little," I said tenderly.

"Yes, I guess. The baby will wake up in several hours and I think you need to go to the store and buy more baby formula," she told me tersely.

I stared at Maya in disbelief, and asked her why she didn't tell me that before I got home. Maya stared daggers at me, a tiny muscle under her lip ticking to signify her displeasure.

Not taking the hint about her mood, I said to her, "Maya, this month's credit card bills were high, and I'm getting the sense that we're living beyond our means."

Maya lunged at me in anger and I could now clearly see that twitch under her lip. Her face was twisted with tremendous anger. She suddenly grasped my elbow, her nails pinching my skin. I jumped backward in pain.

This move seemed to startle Maya and she ran out side, slamming the door behind her. I was in shock and just stood there for several minutes. I decided to go get Maya and apologize. I walked toward the shed in the backyard, as I assumed that was where Maya had run. The shed door was locked and the small windows were dark. I couldn't see anything inside.

I walked around the shed several times and found a small crack in the wall connecting to the foundation. I bent down to peep in through this crack. Bending down on my knees I peeped in. When my eyes started to get used to the faint light inside, I saw something on the floor that had a vague looked like a human shape. I looked closer and saw it was Maya laying in a fetal position on the shed floor. I could hear her crying and asked her to open the door. She didn't respond, just continued crying.

"Maya, we need to get back inside with the baby. Please, open the door!"

I pressed my nose to the door and yelled again. "Maya, I'm sorry. Please open the door!"

I was standing there in the cold with a great sense of terror for the well-being of my wife. *Why did she have this extreme reaction to a small disagreement with me? Why did she run outside and hide?* I felt this episode was like a bad dream, but it wasn't a dream.

I again approached the door and asked, "Maya, please come back home; it's cold outside. Your baby and I need you to come inside." I could hear my voice trembling as I begged. I heard some noises from within the shed and the door opened. I grabbed Maya and gave her a hug, and then I covered her with my jacket and walked her back inside. I was glad this wasn't a nightmare with a bad ending, and I was happy to be back in the warm house.

After this episode I decided not to question Maya about anything she did. She had freedom with her purchases and schedule. I never limited her at school or work, or in any activity she decided to pursue. She was able to finish her undergraduate degree and start her master's degree in social work. Throughout her studies, I helped her with every assignment, and reviewed and corrected every paper she wrote. I did it with dedication and she usually got good grades on her assignments. I saw it as a duty to help my wife and never hesitated in doing so.

Three years after our marriage, I sold my pre-marital home and purchased a custom-made house in Marlboro, New Jersey. Maya said she couldn't live in the house in Long Island and I thought she might want to have a shared ownership in the new house. I didn't mind it because she was my wife and the mother of my child.

I thought Maya would be happier and calmer after I had made the decision to sell my house and purchase a new house together. We selected the building site and the builder offered us many customized options. I let Maya decide everything except the color of the bricks, because she couldn't make it to the meeting where that decision was made.

Maya was terribly upset about the color of the bricks She had requested white bricks and the builder provided white-grey bricks. She was annoyed and started screaming about it.

When Maya is angry, she yells and then violently pulls and pushes anyone standing next to her. I used to get terrified when she got angry — I didn't know how to respond. To make matters worse, I thought that as a man I should react, so I screamed back. My screaming just further aggravated Maya and this angry episode lasted several more hours.

I didn't think the color of the bricks could have such an effect on Maya, but that was another clue that I just didn't understand Maya. Later on she didn't bring the brick color issue up again because the house looked nice with the current brick color, which faded somehow to become a lighter gray.

I had applied for Maya's immigration change to permanent resident on the day we got married. Because of her legal "deportation" status, the permanent resident status change was a complicated issue. I wrote several letters to senators and to my local congressmen, all to no avail.

Four years after our marriage, Maya and I hired a competent law firm to help obtain her permanent resident status. Maya was stressed about this and inflicted her anxiety on me. She once said that in the hospital where she was training she saw immigration officers who handcuffed a patient to be deported. I just brushed off these remarks and didn't understand the depth of emotion underlying these remarks. This was another "proof" of my lack of understanding of Maya, and her feelings and ways of communication. Instead of assuring Maya and talking with her about this, I just brushed off her remarks.

After more than eight years of marriage, Maya got her permanent resident status. This was a relief to Maya and me. She was able to get a job in the same hospital at where she interned for her masters in social work degree. The day she had wished for so badly had arrived, and she called me many times from her work and thanked me for helping her achieve her dream.

Maya was out of the house for many hours every day. She was working and studying at the same time. She was goal driven and applied for a PhD in psychology, which she started studying for right after being accepted to a distance learning school.

Maya took her studies seriously and so did I. I helped her with every document she wrote, and there were many. Maya was aware that her failing dedication to the children might jeopardize her relationship with me, yet it seemed she didn't care. On the contrary, her zeal for work and study didn't stop.

She used to work and study day and night and it seemed she didn't care if the children got hurt or were sick, as long as she was left alone to do her work. She was ever-present in controlling everything to do with the children, though, and she used to call home repeatedly to verify that the children were fed, bathed, and had finished their homework.

When she didn't have night classes or evening double shifts, she came home early and her immediate interaction with our children was to take them shopping. On the other evenings when she was at home, she usually went to her study room to do her assignments. On those days, our house was filled with Maya's repeated requests to calm down our children when their constant talking, playing and fighting with each other, bothered her.

"Just stop screaming!" Maya used to yell, when the children tried to play any noisy game. Several times, my oldest daughter got spanked when she tried to do something that Maya considered off limits. The limits could change from day to day and the guidelines were not set by Maya, which confused our children because they weren't sure what the limits were. When Maya was present, they kept a watchful eye on her reactions.

One evening when Maya came home relatively early, the children were at play under my relaxed and independent supervision.

"You're so mean," I heard my oldest daughter say, this time because Anika had pulled her sister's hair and taken away her iPod.

"What's the matter with you?" I heard Maya yell when she entered the room, holding her briefcase with her purse strapped to her neck. "Let your sister alone, right now!" and then she proceeded to walk quickly towards Ally.

Ally, who was alarmed, froze for a second and then yelled, "Mama, I love you!"

"I love you," but this didn't stop the slap from coming.

"I didn't do it!" Ally yelled in pain and ran crying to her room. I ran after Ally to calm her down but Maya told me not to interfere. She always wanted to handle the children in her own way; I couldn't do anything. When she was with the children I felt sometimes her personality changed and she regressed back to her own childhood.

I knew her childhood had been a bad one. Once I rushed to Maya's room after hearing her screaming "Mama, please do not hit me! Mama, stop!"

I grabbed her and held her tightly. "Maya, what happened?" I asked

Maya moved her head as though she was in a trance. "Mama hit me for nothing"

"Your mama isn't here," I said

Maya opened her eyes and held my hand tightly "Did you hit me?" she asked haltingly.

"Of course not," I replied.

Maya's flashbacks into her past were happening more often as our children got older. One night I heard her screaming, "You're drunk again, Ivan!" and she started crying in her sleep.

I tried to wake her up but couldn't. After several minutes I heard her again yelling. "Do not touch me, you drunk. I'll kill you if you touch me."

I knew it was another nightmare and I didn't try to wake her up. We sometimes had long conversations about her childhood, but she seemed to try to mask any bad memories she had. Maya's childhood memories were mixed. She remembered the good times with her father, but she couldn't understand how come he deserted them suddenly and never contacted them again. She didn't remember her father spanking her, but she did remember her mother spanking her on many occasions.

Maya, in one particular intimate evening, approached me and told me a story about her childhood. She just came over and sat down next to me on the sofa, hugged me and started talking. She remembered seeing a steam locomotive passing daily far away, moving south from the northern direction, and she and her sister usually stopped whatever they were doing, and stared at the train and the people inside. She always felt a desire to take the train and go away to a better life.

One day she started running after the train, and her mother amazement observed her and tried to call her back, but Maya continued running. When she didn't stop, her mother started running after her. When Maya noticed her mother running behind her, staring at her with angry eyes and heard her angrily shouting, "Maya, come back here right now! I said *now!*"

Maya stopped running and fell to the ground. "Mamma, don't hit me! Mamma, don't hit me!" Maya yelled back.

The moment Maya fell to the ground, her mother, holding her shirt tightly, started spanking her. "If you do this again, you will be spanked much harder!" her mother yelled. "Do you want someone to take you away?"

"Yes, Mamma!" Maya answered and got spanked again. Maya then shrugged her shoulders, ignoring the physical pain. "That's all right, Mamma, go on!"

The only thing Maya remembered was getting slapped hard on her face and her mother cruelly leaving her alone in that field next to the train tracks.

I held Maya tightly and gave her a kiss. She started crying loudly. I rarely saw Maya crying and it was a great emotional relief for both of us.

Several years later Maya got her permanent resident status. I felt a great relief as she had always lived in fear of deportation. The permanent resident status was a relief to all of us and she definitely seemed more independent and secure. She was made permanent at work, and she seemed to be more confident and assertive, but on the other hand less appreciative of my efforts to help her.

I started feeling insecure about our marriage, and I felt that this angel I initially met was turning into a devil. I felt that Maya went to school right at the beginning of our marriage because she intended to build herself up for independent living. I started feeling more and more anxiety and I was seeking some assurance from her. I couldn't find any angelic attributes in her anymore. I remembered that she'd left her first husband with ease and no remorse. I was worried that she might do the same to me.

She seemed to enjoy being at work more than being at home. She started buying fashionable clothes and shoes, and tried to keep up with the latest fashion. She dressed very well for work and spent considerable time in the morning putting on makeup. I asked her why she didn't dress up when we went out and she claimed that we go nowhere together.

We used to go out to eat in restaurants once or twice a week, and from time to time also go for short vacations. At least once a year we went on a long vacation overseas.

When I asked Maya to tell me "I love you" she couldn't say it, and gave an explanation that it was because of me.

When Maya was finishing up her studies for her PhD in psychology, she started to talk to me with complete disrespect and sometimes with absolute contempt. Later on, Maya started asking me to keep a distance and couldn't look into my eyes. My anxiety about a pending breakup was growing and no signals were given from Maya to relax this anxiety.

One evening, Maya came back late and I rushed to hug her. "I love you," I said.

"I know, I know!" Maya yelled suddenly with a tremendous amount of anger and impatience noticeable in her high-pitched response.

"So, are you my love?" I asked affectionately.

There was no doubt that Maya was offended by this question, but she said nothing.

Maya turned a little toward me and then began staring at me with marked impatience, in a way she had never looked at me before. It was as though I was a creature from another planet. I shuddered and moved my eyes away.

There was something very mean and peculiar in the way she was staring at me. It felt at first as though she was staring into a void, as though I wasn't there at all. Then, I felt her contempt.

She turned her face away from me, and I felt my face turning red. I had just undergone a traumatic and shameful event. It felt like a deep stab in my heart and I couldn't hear my heart beat, or feel my pulse. Maya's responses and behavior confirmed my suspicions that something was very wrong.

Later that evening Maya asked, "Did you finish checking Ally's homework?"

I was startled and moved to sit in the chair in the dining room. I answered in a weak and breaking voice, "Yes, I did. What else do you want to ask me?"

Maya straightened her gaze toward me and with a cold and heavily accented voice said, "David, I hope you've taken the garbage out, otherwise the rest of the evening won't be pleasant for you!"

I was sitting there, staring at her, expecting some kind words. Instead I got something quite different, and I just gazed blankly at her. I didn't reply, as though I didn't hear what she said. I just sat there gazing at her face.

"Are you going to answer me?" Maya asked, somehow with both impatience and disinterest.

In reply I just sank down in my chair, put my hands on the table and gazed back at her with dismay. Maya returned my look with her eyes burning and signs of her impending explosion of anger. Looking at her, I finally got the picture that my 11 years of life with her were coming to an end.

CHAPTER TEN

Trial Continues

The court officer suddenly jumped from his chair, and I felt as though Maya had just leaped forward and rushed with anger toward me. I woke up from my deep thoughts and I saw the court officer in front of me. He then asked me to return and escorted me back to Judge Killmen's court, and it seemed as though I hadn't left at all. I was back sitting on my chair and the Judge entered the court right after the court officer yelled the traditional "All Rise." "Here comes the court's queen," I said to myself. Judge Killmen continued her trial.

JUDGE: "Are there any other events of domestic violence that you would like me to know about?"

MAYA: "I called the Marlboro police a number of times because I saw his car next to our house, more than once because I felt somebody was following me. I asked them to wait for me at the house so that I could walk into it safely, make sure that everything was safe. I know so many officers in Marlboro police department, including Captain Marks, Chief of Police. Sgt. Dump also knows our family very well, and so does Sgt. Feldshoe, because my husband also constantly calls them. He apparently has a habit of calling the Marlboro police to try to find out where I am.

This is too much. Judge Killmen and my lawyer should both object to this blatant perjury. How ridiculous to say that I would call the police to find out where she was and what she was doing, while I was under a civil restraining order! How can this Judge rightly allow testimony regarding police officers that are not present? I felt I was sinking down, down into the chair, melting into the room like a nobody. But the charade just went on and on.

JUDGE: "So the police have been to your home how many times would you say?"

MAYA: "By now, I think it's about forty, between them being in my house and me being in the Marlboro police station."

JUDGE: "And in how long a period of time?"

MAYA: "That's since December of last year, up to now."

JUDGE: "Is there anything else you would like me to know before Todd Prone asks you questions? If you need a minute to look at your notes, that's fine."

MAYA: "Yes, I just feel like I can't move on with my life because David tries to control every step I take. He tries to intimidate me. You know that from the first time I actually saw you, your honor. It started back then and it continues. I'm afraid to take a step without looking over my shoulder.

"I ask my coworkers to walk me out of every place of employment because he either waits for me or he follows me. Any interaction that we have with him, even if it's in court, he'll make sure that he calls me horrible names.

"When he was ordered by Judge Irish to attend reunification therapy with the children, he would bring some strange person into the session, to wait in the waiting room. This was some man who had nothing to do with us. I went to Marlboro police about this but there was nothing they could do about it because they said David was entitled to bring whoever he wanted. I don't even know the man. I don't know what his intentions are.

"I feel like it's just getting worse and worse, to the point that as we get closer to divorce, he feels that he's losing control and he's going to punish me for whatever reason because I left him. I seriously believe David is going to hurt me. He calculated precisely what my life insurance is, to the penny. I didn't even know that amount.

"He also abuses my family. He calls constantly. My sister travels and she was working in Latvia where we're from. He makes sure he calls there and threatens her. He calls my the Ukraine, threatening my dad who is 75 years old, because he said my dad owes him some money."

TODD: "Your honor, I object. This is hearsay. Her her dad is in Ukraine and can't testify."

JUDGE: "I'll sustain that objection. But, Maya, he has called your father?

The Judge continues even after she sustains the objection it just didn't make sense.

MAYA "Yes, he called my father. My mother takes care of our kids now and he passed by, not in the last month because we had a restraining order, but prior to that. He passes by the house because he knows that she's there and, you know, she takes kids for a walk or whatever. He'll make sure that he opens the window and yells something horrible to my mom. I don't know what to do."

JUDGE: "Do you have a copy of your civil restraining order?"

MAYA: "I do."

Now the testimony of Maya sounded more like a rant, the story of a woman with intense paranoia that hadn't even one element of truth. But the Judge still allowed it. It was as if she had already convicted me. The Judge knows that I do not speak Russian at all, while Maya's parents speak no English, but she continues to let this crazy process go on. Now I was thinking this Judge must have personal issues against men — or at this man, for she definitely gave me no break at all.

JUDGE: "Do you happen to have a copy of any order regarding custody and parenting time with you there?"

MAYA: "You know what; I didn't bring that because I didn't know –"

JUDGE: "Okay. I can get to that."

MAYA: "David has not seen his children alone since May. He only sees our kids through the therapy meetings."

JUDGE: "Okay. So since this order was filed on February 22nd, has he tried to call you?"

MAYA: "Yes, even after Judge Irish entered the order that he isn't allowed calling or emailing me."

JUDGE: "So he violated the provision that he should not have any communication with you."

MAYA: "Yes."

JUDGE: "Has he violated the provision that he's not to have any communication with any of your coworkers?"

MAYA: "Yes, constantly."

JUDGE: "And since February, you say he has stalked you?"

MAYA: "Yeah, absolutely."

JUDGE: "He has been seen at your place of employment?"

MAYA: "Yes."

JUDGE: "All right, is there anything else you would like me to know, Maya?"

MAYA: "Just the fact that I called the Marlboro police back in December when David hit me, and I told them he had weapons in the house. I asked the police to remove the guns from the house. When David came to the Marlboro police department, I was notified he had asked for a letter of good conduct so that he could get his weapons back.

"I asked what this meant. They said that since he's trying to go to trial, there will be a court hearing in the prosecutor's office. And you know, the weapons might be given back to him if they decide he's capable at some point to have them back. So they told me to write a letter to the prosecutor's office explaining why I don't want him to have weapons back. I did, and I don't know what happened with that. But I really don't want David to access to any weapons."

JUDGE: "Now, you said he hit you in December?"

MAYA: "Yes."

JUDGE: "December of last year?"

MAYA: "December 29th of last year."

JUDGE: "What happened there?"

MAYA: "We didn't live together like a couple any more but we lived in the same house. I had already filed for divorce and he was just behaving in a horrible manner. He was extremely abusive verbally, and wouldn't leave me alone.

"One morning when we were getting ready to go to New York he said some really nasty things to me, calling me names like prostitute and whore and all that stuff. My daughter was right there. My daughter was ten at the time. She got into an argument with him about it, telling him not to call her mom those names. And when he tried to hit her or push her, I stood in between. So instead of hitting her, he hit me."

JUDGE: "Were you injured when he hit you?"

MAYA: "He hit me on the head, with his open hand. I didn't go to the hospital."

JUDGE: "Did it hurt you?"

MAYA: "Yes, absolutely."

JUDGE: "Is there anything else you would like me to know before Todd Prone asks you questions in cross examination?"

MAYA: " No, but maybe I'll remember something."

JUDGE: "Okay, if you do, you can tell me after he's done."

MAYA: "Okay."

JUDGE: "All right, Todd Prone, cross examination."

Of course Maya didn't mention her physical and verbal assaults on me, her endless shouting, calling me names in Russian and insulting me. She didn't mention her kicking, scratching and punching when she was in her angry mood. She would not mention that she physically abused our own daughter, always using a heavy hand to punish her. I myself started to feel the signs of abuse, not only by my spouse and her family but by this judge. The tightness in my stomach increased and strong pains moved through the muscles of my hands and legs as my pulse raced. I couldn't think clearly. I was overwhelmed by my lack of control and inadequacy in handing this. I felt small as an ant, ready to be crushed. For several moments I started to believe that what Maya was saying, that the whole dismal affair, was entirely my fault. I wanted to get up and leave but I was frozen by my muscles, my mind and the law. There was no other option for me but accept the situation as it was. I decided to put my faith in this young lawyer and hoped he would be able to expose the truth in his cross examination of Maya. I watched them with fading hope.

TODD: "Maya, you just stated to the Judge on December 29th, that David and you had an argument, correct?"

MAYA: "I didn't have an argument with David. David was calling me names, yes."

TODD: "So you weren't arguing with David. You weren't screaming at David."

MAYA: "As a result, I might have screamed later on when everything got worse."

TODD: "Okay. So you were having an argument with David."

MAYA: "Eventually we did, because he kept calling me names and was pushing my daughter, yes."

TODD: "And you testified that he called you a prostitute?"

MAYA: "Yes."

TODD: "And you testified that he hit you on the head?"

MAYA: "I not only testified; I have a police report stating that."

TODD: "Okay. During the course of this argument, did you ever threaten David?"

MAYA: "Not as I recall."

TODD: "Did you ever tell David that you were going to, quote: 'fucking bury him?'"

MAYA: "Not as I recall. However, in the heat of the argument when I was very angry and protective of my kids and myself, I might have said something like that. I don't remember."

TODD: "Okay. So you don't know. You're not sure."

MAYA: "I don't recall. It was about a year ago."

TODD: " If you did say something like that, just hypothetical, what does "I'm going to fucking bury you" mean?"

MAYA: "I don't know, because I don't remember saying that."

TODD: "Judge, I would like to have this marked as defense Exhibit—1."

JUDGE: "What is it?"

TODD: "It's a recording of the argument that took place on December 29th recorded by David with a digital recording device."

JUDGE: "So we'll have that be D-1, a recording of an argument on December 29th? How long is the recording?"

TODD: "The segment with the quote is about 10 seconds long."

JUDGE: "Can you play it on that device? I don't know how else we're going to play it."

TODD: "Yes, I can play it on this."

JUDGE: "Okay.

TODD: "I would like you to listen to this, Maya."

Recording: *"I'm going to fucking bury you.... I'm going to fucking bury you!"*

TODD: "Was that you on the tape saying that you were going to fucking bury him?"

MAYA: "I don't know."

TODD: "You're not sure if that was you screaming at him?"

MAYA: "I don't know if it's my voice, no. Does it have a date? Because it was never documented, or filed anywhere or with the Marlboro police."

TODD: "Do you have the whole recording, David?"

JUDGE: "How long is the whole recording?"

DAVID: "About five minutes. Maya was yelling at me about money next to my daughter Ally and then she pushed me. I initially didn't respond to her questioning about money in our joint account because I have funded it for ten years. Her new source of income was going to a different bank account. However, I didn't touch that account. It is sad that it happened in front of my children. I have the whole segment ready to play when you request it to be heard."

TODD: "So David never called you a prostitute on December 29th, did he?"

MAYA: "Yes, he did."

TODD: "And he never did hit you on that night, did he?"

MAYA: "Yes, he did. Please read the police report from that date."

TODD: "Was there any indication on the tape that David hit you on the head?"

MAYA: "I don't know when David recorded that. David had a tendency to record everything, every time we had any type of argument or conversation. Does it have the date? How do you know when it was recorded?"

TODD: "Maya, did you not tell him that you were going to fucking bury him?"

MAYA: "From what you're hearing of the arguments that took place on that day, I don't know what date it was."

TODD: "Maya, did you tell him that you were going to fucking bury him?"

JUDGE: "It would go a lot quicker if you could tell us, was that your voice that said the words -I'm going to bury you."

MAYA: "It must have been my voice."

JUDGE: "Okay, next question."

TODD: "Maya, you also stated you didn't know David was a writer."

MAYA: "Yes, I didn't know that."

TODD: "Okay. You've been married for ten years, correct?"

MAYA: "Eleven."

TODD: "And you're aware that David has had no less than probably eighty published works?"

MAYA: "No, I had no idea."

TODD: "So you've lived with David for eleven years, been with him for eleven years, and you didn't know that he was a writer with eighty published works."

MAYA: "What works did he publish?"

TODD: "Political essays."

MAYA: "Not that I'm aware of. I know he's a computer programmer who spends a lot of time on the computer writing his software. I know he was writing a journal about our relationship. But I had no idea that David spends a lot of time writing something else."

TODD: "Now, you also stated, Maya that you received that manuscript that was referred to in January."

MAYA: "Correct."

TODD: "January of this year, correct?"

MAYA: "Correct."

TODD: "Have you ever seen Ms. Mally, the counselor, Maya?"

MAYA: "I saw her once very briefly for David's session, which he asked me to attend and I did for about fifteen minutes."

TODD: "Okay. And that was sometime in November or October of last year, around that date?"

MAYA: "Right before I filed for divorce, when we had a lot of relationship problems."

TODD: "So it was before that you claim that you were given this copy of the manuscript though, correct?"

MAYA: "Yes, that was before."

TODD: "Okay. And at the time that you met with Ms. Mally, she in fact had presented you with a copy of this manuscript, had she not?"

MAYA: "No, she didn't. She presented me with a copy of the manuscript that David wrote about me and him and our relationship in the last number of years. "

TODD: "But you were presented with a portion of the manuscript at that point, correct?"

MAYA: "No, that wasn't a portion of that manuscript. It was very similar writing about how we met and what our relationship was and how David felt about me."

TODD: "So you knew about a portion of the manuscript regarding the plane incident before January."

MAYA: "That was a completely separate manuscript."

TODD: "Okay. You've also alleged today that David calls you at work. That he shows up at work. That he harasses your coworkers. Have you brought any' phone records with you today?"

MAYA: "I didn't bring phone records. We didn't record them at my home, but I have a letter from my work, from my place of employment and my coworkers."

TODD: "Did you bring the person who wrote that letter?"

MAYA: "No, I didn't bring that person because I do not want to involve anybody in person."

JUDGE: "Can I tell you something? You're going to make the trial last five times longer than it needs to. The answer is no. It doesn't matter why. No is fine."

MAYA: "Okay."

JUDGE: "And the next question, answer with a yes or no."

TODD: "Did you bring any of the people who claimed to have been harassed by David?"

MAYA: "I have letters from these people."

TODD: "So that's a no."

JUDGE: "So the answer is no, okay. Next question!"

TODD: "Did you bring the doctor who you claim received nasty phone calls from David? Is he here today?"

MAYA: "I have a letter from him."

TODD: "So none of the people whom you claim were harassed are here today."

MAYA: "No. Actually, yes, two people, my sister and my mom, my witnesses. They're here."

TODD: "Well, none of your coworkers though."

MAYA: "No, because –"

TODD: "So none of the coworkers who claim to have seen David outside your work, and none of the coworkers who apparently received these phone calls are here today either, correct?"

MAYA: "I could give you all the phone numbers and the names of those people. You can confirm."

TODD: "And you stated you work in a jail."

MAYA: "Yes, I do."

TODD: "You also stated that David had shown up at work."

MAYA: "He did."

TODD: "Okay. You also stated there were video cameras outside work."

MAYA: "As I stated before to Judge Killmen, at the jail there are video cameras, not at the Hospital."

TODD: "But you also stated that David showed up at the jail."

MAYA: "He did in January of last year."

TODD: "And at jail, there's obviously security systems, and lots of security outside of jail. You said it yourself –"

MAYA: "No, inside."

TODD: "How about outside? There are no video cameras outside?"

MAYA: "Yes, there are."

TODD: "So if David was to arrive at your work and your coworkers were to see him, there would obviously be a video of David, correct?"

MAYA: "Maybe. I didn't check with DOC officers."

TODD: "Did you bring those videos with you today?"

MAYA: "I explained to you, I didn't check with DOC officers."

TODD: "So Maya, basically at this point what you're telling me is that all the people who apparently were the recipients of harassment from David aren't here to testify."

MAYA: "I'm the main recipient of David's harassment and I'm here."

TODD: "You have no phone records and you have no video, correct?"

MAYA: "We don't record phone conversations."

JUDGE: "It has already been asked and answered so let's just keep moving."

TODD: "Maya, you stated on July 14th, I believe, that David followed you?"

MAYA: "He cut me off."

TODD: "Okay. He cut you off and then you said you dialed pound 77, which is the erratic driver hotline."

MAYA: "Yes."

TODD: "Okay. Are you aware that on July 14th, the same time you filed that report, David was actually in a therapy session with your children?"

MAYA: "No. Because I came into Marlboro police station after the therapy session with my children!"

TODD: "You came to the Marlboro station after. But on July 14th, the date that you made the report, —"

MAYA: "The same day, I came into Marlboro police station –"

TODD: "Are you aware that on that date, he was in a therapy session?"

MAYA: "I'm very aware because I was right there. We had an appointment with Dr. Psylie. I dropped my children off there and picked them up later. I dropped them off at home. David followed me back home. I sat in the car and then drove to Elizabeth, to my work. He followed me on Route 9, cut me off at Route 9 and intersection of 516 West. I continued going to work. I became extremely emotional and fearful, and called pound 77. I called my work, and asked them for the day off. I returned back to Marlboro police department and filed the report. I remember the day very well."

TODD: "Maya, you told the police what happened, you filed the report and told them that the incident happened at a particular time. You gave them a time."

MAYA: "Yes."

TODD: "The time that you gave the police was the time that he was at counseling, correct?"

MAYA: "No, the time I gave the police was when I was driving and David was right behind me."

TODD: "Maya, in reference to your previous restraining order, the December 29th incident that you allege happened to you, that we've talked about—"

MAYA: "It did happen. I don't allege."

TODD: "You didn't file for your restraining order."

MAYA: "I was offered to do so by the Marlboro police department and I refused at the time because I wanted to finish the divorce peacefully and just to continue with that. I didn't want David to be removed from the house. I wanted him to leave on his own."

TODD: "What eventually you did go and file for; — you were turned down for a restraining order, on more than one occasion, correct?"

MAYA: "On January 8th, yes, right here."

TODD: "And then you went and filed for another restraining order, correct?"

MAYA: "In the Marlboro police department, correct, January 26th, early this year."

TODD: "Okay. January 6th."

MAYA: "26th."

TODD: "And you also received the complaint on the 26th. So a full month after December 29th, did you file for a restraining order based on the December 29th incident?"

MAYA: "No, it wasn't that incident. It was many incidents after that. If you want me to go over what happened since then, I will."

TODD: "Let me ask you this, Maya. You also filed for this restraining order after your mother was served with the complaint. Correct?"

MAYA: "It had nothing to do with that."

TODD: "And you also received the complaint. How many days after you filed this restraining order did you file this complaint?"

MAYA: "I don't remember but that was another day of harassing me and my mother by filing criminal charges against us."

TODD: "So it's just a coincidence that the date you received this complaint, that your mother received this complaint, you went and filed a restraining order for something that had happened on December 29th."

MAYA: "I did ask for a restraining order and, yes, I wasn't granted one."

TODD: "You stated that David hacked your computer records."

MAYA: "Yes, he did. I have proof right here."

TODD: "Are you aware that David was undergoing an IRS audit?"

MAYA: "It's not just David who was going through that. We are, as a family. It's a joint tax return."

TODD: "Okay. So the family is going through an IRS audit?"

MAYA: "Me and him, yes, for the last two years."

TODD: "Are you both preparing for this IRS audit?"

MAYA: "I did all the work."

TODD: "You did all the work? David didn't contribute at all to this IRS audit?"

MAYA: "No. I hired the attorney from DBCDA, Mr. Pomerantz, he's dealing with that issue. David wasn't. We're dealing with that issue, also with Judge Irish."

TODD: "As part of this IRS audit, they go into your financial records. Correct? There's an accounting for it. There are checking accounts, credit cards, and such."

MAYA: "No."

TODD: "No?"

MAYA: "I presented to them whatever they requested, and that wasn't part of it. No."

TODD: "Well, how about as part of your divorce proceedings? Has the Judge asked for any financial information?"

MAYA: "We were provided interrogatories, custody interrogatories and financial interrogatories, yes."

TODD: "Did the Judge request any financial information from David?"

MAYA: "That was part of the discovery. It was due September—"

TODD: "Credit card bills?"

MAYA: "September 1st. David has not provided anything to date."

TODD: "That's not true. Did the Judge request credit card bills?"

MAYA: "Not from me."

TODD: "Did she request them from David?"

MAYA: "Who's she? I don't know who she—"

TODD: "Judge Irish, I'm sorry, Judge Irish. Did Judge Irish request credit card information?"

MAYA: "I don't know what he requested from David."

TODD: "Well, did you make your travel plans on your American Express card? The travel plans that you referred to."

MAYA: "How is this relevant? This was done through my computer. The point is, David wasn't privy to that information."

TODD: "Just a very simple question. Were the travel plans paid for with an American Express card?"

MAYA: "Yes."

TODD: "Has David, at any point, paid the bills for that American Express card?"

MAYA: "No."

TODD: "Never?"

MAYA: "No. This is my credit card. It's only in my name."

TODD: "He has never given you one to pay the bills?"

MAYA: "The answer is no."

TODD: "Maya, you recently finished school. How long have you been going to school?"

MAYA: "I'm still in school."

TODD: "You're still in school?"

MAYA: "Yes, I'm working on my dissertation."

TODD: "Okay. Who is paying for school?"

MAYA: "I'm paying for school."

TODD: "Did you receive any student loans?"

JUDGE: "Todd Prone, I'm trying to be patient. Where are you going with this?"

TODD: "Well, Maya is claiming that David had no attachment to this American Express bill. The computer hacking that she's alleging is this American Express bill that David provided to Judge Irish as part of the divorce proceedings."

MAYA: "Where did David get this information?"

JUDGE: "So, he paid the American Express bill. Okay. So you can bring that out in his testimony. Obviously, you're not getting anywhere with this testimony. She said he has hacked into her computer and has information concerning various travel plans that would not be a part of paying a bill."

TODD: "I'll stop on that question."

Again this Judge was directing my lawyer and his cross-examination and he didn't have my lawyer didn't have the nerve to stand up for his points. Just as I was starting to feel my lawyer was persuasive and was going after some of the inconsistent and baseless points of the testimony, he got weak in the knees again. I didn't know why he agreed with everything

Judge had decided. It seemed that he was just resigned to the fact that this judge would decide whatever he wants and ignore any points he tried to make. He seemed to be afraid of the judge and my spouse's lawyer. I didn't expect this from him. The Judge was cutting him off and telling him what to do rather consistently. I felt the urge to get up and run. The trial was like a dream from Dante's hell, and I was in the center of it, descending into the lower rings of fire and ice. Then there was Maya, going on and on, making it up as she went along.

TODD: "The allegation in the complaint is that the defendant called your house, spoke with your sister and your children and said that bad things were going to happen."

MAYA: "Yes."

TODD: "Today, you testified that he called your house and said that he was going to kill you. Correct?"

MAYA: "No, I said he told my sister that he's going to kill her and because my daughter was on another line, he told my daughter to give a message to me. He said to tell her mother that something bad is going to happen to her."

TODD: "However, your complaint only states that David said bad things are going to happen to you."

MAYA: "Sometimes things do not get reported or recorded as they were said. Sometimes things get missed in translation because those are like three different papers by the time I got to the hearing officer and everything else."

TODD: "Well, in your opinion is there a the difference between 'I'm going to kill you' and 'bad things are going to happen?'"

MAYA: "My sister is here and she's going to testify to what happened."

TODD: "Nothing further, Your Honor."

JUDGE: "All right, why don't we call in your first witness? We'll call your mother first with the interpreter."

MAYA: "Yes."

JUDGE: "What's your mother's name?"

MAYA: "Ingrid Getall."

JUDGE: "Spell her last name for me."

MAYA: "G-e-t-a-l-l."

JUDGE: "If we could slide another chair down for the interpreter that would be great."

TODD: "Your Honor, I'm sorry, I have to object to this witness's testimony. She's not mentioned in either this TRO complaint or prior TRO complaints. Nowhere is it alleged that she had anything to do with this incident whatsoever. I'm not sure that she can offer as to what happened on this particular occasion or on the previous occasions."

JUDGE: "Well, I won't know, either, until I hear from her."

TODD: "Okay."

JUDGE: "Actually, we'll have the witness in the box and the interpreter next to her. Okay, great. Ms. Getall, Would you please come to this witness box here. Remain standing, and I request the interpreter to please raise her right hand and state her name, spelling your last name."

INTERPRETER: "My name is Vera Gutin. G-u-t-i-n.

JUDGE: "Thank you for being here this morning. I request the witness to please place her left hand on the Bible, and raise her right hand. Yes, please state your name."

INGRID: "Ingrid Getall."

JUDGE: "Thank you very much, please be seated."

Why is Maya's mother even testifying here? The judge should know that for a crime to be considered a domestic violence offense, the perpetrator and victim must have a personal relationship at present or in the past. I hadn't had contact with her mother for years. How could I have spoken to her? Maya didn't receive the alleged phone call, the main subject matter of this TRO, so why was this process in motion? The Judge also allowed converting a hearing on a complaint alleging one act of harassment by telephone into a hearing on other acts of domestic violence, which are not even alleged in the complaint. This was fundamental violation of due process, and I could do nothing. If my lawyer had already lost his nerve, how would any truth be revealed?

TODD: Your Honor—

JUDGE: "If you have any objection to a particular question, then by all means you can voice your objection to the question. But she's here as a witness and we'll hear from her."

JUDGE: "So, Ms. Getall, you're the mother of the plaintiff?"

INGRID: "Yes."

JUDGE: "Are you currently living with the plaintiff?"

INGRID: "Yes."

JUDGE: "How long have you been living with the plaintiff?"

INGRID: "I come and go. I come here every half a year."

JUDGE: "How how many years have you done this?"

INGRID: "Eleven years."

JUDGE: "So part of that time included when they lived together?"

INGRID: "Only in the last year I didn't live with them, with both of them. Till then I used to live with both of them. He was present, too."

JUDGE: "And then he separated from the plaintiff in January of this year. Is that correct?"

INGRID: "Yes."

JUDGE: "Okay. So I'll ask the plaintiff, what questions do you have for your mother?"

MAYA: "I just want my mom to explain what happens when she sees him, or you know, what phone calls she receives from him, or how she feels threatened by him and what she has observed through the year basically."

JUDGE: "Well, let me try to break that down. Since January of this year, have you observed the defendant or his vehicle at or around the residence where you live with the plaintiff?"

INGRID: "Yes."

JUDGE: "How many times?"

INGRID: "I didn't count but very often when I'm cleaning something outside, he's passing by. I'm taking a walk with the children outside and he's passing by. He's shouting. He's yelling."

JUDGE: "So, when he passes by and he sees you, he'll shout something?"

INGRID: "Yes, he usually shouts. He says, 'I'll kill you, you Russian prostitute.'"

If I do not speak Russian and Ingrid is using an interpreter what language did I use to yell at her? Sign language? The Judge didn't get it and we continued as usual.

JUDGE: "When was the last time you heard him shout something to you?"
INGRID: "The last time was over the phone. But you know I don't keep the records."
JUDGE: "I don't need exact dates. I'm just asking generally. Approximately how many times has he shouted something since January?"
INGRID: "About five times. Not to mention the times when he just came to pick up the children, because he was usually accompanied by police."
JUDGE: "Okay. So these were times when he didn't have arrangements to pick up the children."
INGRID: "Yes, yes."
TODD: "I'm sorry, Your Honor, could you clarify? Did he have permission to pick up the children or didn't he? I didn't understand."
JUDGE: "No, these five times were not times when he was picking up the children, when he was shouting and driving by."

Again, the Judge was answering on behalf of the witness. This trial was sounding like a lynch mob of angry women conducted by the judge, and I seemed to symbolize all men who have wronged them.

JUDGE: "How often since January of this year would you say he has called the house?"
INGRID: "In the beginning, my daughter changed the phone number. There was silence in the house. Nobody called. Then he started calling. In the beginning, he was talking. Then he didn't say anything. He

would just keep silent then drop the receiver. Then I just wouldn't pick up the phone and left the answering machine on."

JUDGE: "When was the last time you heard his voice at the other end of the phone?"

INGRID: "It was somewhere in the middle of May because I left at the end of May, and then I came back on August 26th."

JUDGE: "What did you hear him say in May?"

INGRID: "He said that my daughter is crazy and that he'll kill her and that she's a prostitute, that she's a bitch and other dirty words. And he didn't feel uncomfortable to say that in the presence of his children."

If she's using an interpreter in this trial and I do not speak her language, how does the Judge think this conversation went through?

JUDGE: "Do you feel that your daughter is in danger?"
INGRID: "Yes."
JUDGE: "Do you have any other questions for your mother?"
MAYA: "No."
JUDGE: "All right, Todd Prone, cross-examination."
TODD: "You said that David appeared at your house five times."
INGRID: "Yes, he was passing by as I was taking a walk. It's not that he just came to the house. We were outside with the children or I was outside."
TODD: "So he would drive by."
INGRID: "He was driving and he was yelling through the window."
TODD: "So he wouldn't stop?"
INGRID: "He would slow down. He would roll down the window and shout."
TODD: "What kind of car does David drive?"
INGRID: "He has a white car, it's a new car. It's long and white. He bought it quite recently."
TODD: "And you claim that he calls the house and hangs up the phone."
INGRID: "Yes, in the beginning. Yes, in the beginning and—"

TODD: "Well, my question is how you know that it's him? You don't know it's him, do you?"

INGRID: "But we didn't receive calls, we haven't received such calls before that. Whoever calls usually leaves a message."

TODD: "Well, my question is why did you assumed it was him?"

INGRID: "Who else would do that? Because my daughter changed the phone number and then he started calling."

TODD: "Your daughter changed the phone number?"

INGRID: "Yes."

TODD: "Did you give the phone number to David?"

INGRID: "He can learn anything he wants. He calls everywhere. He wants to know everything. He calls all my daughter's doctors. He called the school of music. He called everywhere."

This is a mother who will easily commit perjury, because in America you can do it, but back home they would send her to jail for committing perjury, She was ready to do anything needed to gain her daughter's goals here in the new promised land, but Judge Killmen doesn't see it that way.

TODD: "Did your daughter list her phone number with the phone company?"

JUDGE: "I don't know. Why you're asking that question of the mother?"

TODD: "Your Honor, I'm done with that line of questioning."

I was surprised by Todd's decision to terminate the questioning. The thought crossed my mind that he was just a young lawyer without much experience who realized he couldn't do much here. However, I suddenly caught a glimpse of a well-dressed man, who seemed to be known by the court staff and was conversing with the court clerk while the trial was going on. That man was frequently looking at his watch and signaling Todd. I later learned that this man was Todd's Boss, the man who was supposed to be here, to defend me. Time is money especially in the legal world. No business is like the legal business; it has every element, suspense, money, showmanship, drama, tragedy, deception, and some truth and the hard process to achieve the truth.

JUDGE: "Okay."

TODD: "You said you lived with your daughter since January?"

INGRID: "No, I came on December 1st."

TODD: "December 1st, of last year."

TODD: "And your daughter filed for divorce in the middle of December, correct?"

INGRID: "Yes."

TODD: "And you've lived with her ever since, correct?"

INGRID: "I left for Latvia at the end of May and I came back on August 26th."

TODD: "Are you planning to live with your daughter permanently?"

JUDGE: "Don't answer the question. Please tell her not to answer the question. What's the relevance of that?"

TODD: "Well, it's bias, Your Honor. I believe they want him out of the house, both the mother and the sister at this point."

JUDGE: "They're in the middle of a divorce so she's in the residence. I don't see where that bias would be. And certainly, I don't want David to potentially use this type of information to harm her chances of staying or question her visa or what have you. So I'll not force her to answer that question."

TODD: "If you're not a resident of this country, are you here legally?"

JUDGE: "Ask the question but tell her not to answer it."

TODD: "Okay. I'll stop that line of questioning."

JUDGE: "Okay, next question."

TODD: "Do you believe that if your daughter is successful here today, she's going to get custody of the children?"

JUDGE: "Tell her not to answer the question. That's an objectionable question. Again, if you want to make that as part of your argument, then you can make that as part of your argument."

TODD: "I'll withdraw the question."

JUDGE: "It's an unfair question of this witness."

TODD: "Nothing further, Your Honor."

JUDGE: "Okay, thank you, Todd Prone. Do you have any other questions of the mother? No, okay, thank you, you can step down. And you can remain in Judge Killmen's court. But I don't believe we need the interpreter at this point."

At a glance I looked at everyone in this courtroom assessing what they were thinking about me. There was a lady whose piercing eyes were burning with anger and my fingers felt a light tremor when our eyes met. This lady moved her hand to the front of her face. I didn't understand her gesture, and I scanned her face again. She was just tired, not angry, I thought to myself.

Suddenly, I felt an odd start of memory, and my thoughts automatically reverted to an incident just several months ago, when Ingrid was present in her daughter's break-up show of her marriage. Ingrid was there, dressed up and ready for the show she knew was going to happen. That was a Saturday morning nine months before this day.

I got up and unlatched the door to my bedroom, opened my dresser and retrieved the document the police had given me the other day. Strange to say, I realized that the previous night I had become a declared unwanted spouse, and I felt calm without any trace of the delirium of the night before, following the ordeal I had with my spouse's mother. I felt no fear or panic, just calm.

My movements across the room were slow and precise, as though I felt strong enough to face whatever was going to happen. I felt that I was stepping into the next stage of this farce.

"This is the day of reckoning," I muttered to myself. I had finally began to understand that my marriage was over, but that concept had taken a long time to hit me. I had hoped there was still a chance, but realized without much in the way of financial resources left, my chances were weakening day by day.

I dressed in my new jeans and a new polo shirt, and looked at the tape-recorder on the dresser. After a second of hesitation, I shoved it into my pants pocket. I quietly unlatched the door of my bedroom, walked toward the stairs stood there for a second. For me, it felt like I was going into a danger zone — to enemy territory. That the first floor was covered with mines aimed at me.

I walked down the stairs and glanced into the living room. Maya was standing there with her back to me, talking to her mother. My children were playing quietly in my office. I quickly slipped into the kitchen and grabbed something to eat. Maya acted like I didn't exit, pretending she didn't hear me.

Too soon for me, she came into the kitchen and her mother walked headed to the office to be with the children. Maya was dressed in tight black jeans, a turtle neck sweater and a yellow Gap hat — all of it seem new and just out of the package.

It was already nine o'clock, and the sun was in full view from the kitchen window. This bathed the room in sunlight, so I went to switch off the light. I heard Maya's nervous cough, as though she was trying to clear her throat. It was the same nervous tick she'd had for many years. In a strong and demanding voice Maya asked me to turn the light back on.

I switched it back on without saying a word, then walked over to the toaster and shoved a slice of bread into it.

"Did you pay for it?" Maya taunted in her blunt, demanding accent. I felt the question was just meant to demean me in front of my children, so I didn't respond.

Maya walked straight on towards me in an intimidating manner. She stopped just to my left and slightly behind me and asked again, "How much money did you withdraw from the Sovereign Bank account?"

"I took back the one thousand dollars I gave you to buy the dog," I answered hesitantly. Strangely this wasn't the response she was hoping for. I don't think she expected me to withdraw money from the account.

"How much money?" Maya paused and then continued. "I need the exact number from that account. *How much money did you withdraw?*" Maya raised her voice to a scream.

I felt cornered and I wanted to insist on my innocence, but I just stepped back and shrugged my shoulders. I felt like green soldier under intense attack. The only thing I could do was take cover or escape. *I'll never surrender,* I was thinking as I insisted on keeping quiet and not responding to her.

"I'm asking you again!"

"I can take whatever sum I need; it *is* a joint account. No? I've funded that account for the last ten years with my paychecks. Now, the moment you start getting your paychecks you funnel your income into a secret, private account," I answered with a sigh, perplexed at the sudden stroke of courage I displayed.

"I told you, I wrote bills from the account!"

Sure she wrote checks from the account, and I knew it was her last-ditch effort to empty out our joint account. I'd closed all the joint credit cards accounts already but had left this one account open, though I stopped the automatic deposits.

"How much money did *you* take?" I asked Maya sarcastically.

"I told you I wrote bills from the account! How much money did you withdraw from that account?" Maya was now yelling. I was just standing there silently. I smiled as I started to think calmly again. *Yes, this was her attempt to empty out our joint account and she was angry because she was too late. I beat her to it!* I looked at her, hoping to see some sign that she intended to stop yelling at me in front of our children.

There was no compassionate sign, only anger from her. I was already prepared for her next step, though. I started to feel my legs shaking, as the muscles of my stomach tightened. I could hardly breathe. The next move I expected, based on her facial expressions and body language, was I physical violence. W-h-at?" I heard myself stuttering. I stood there recognizing that fear taking over. I rested my elbow on the door handle, as though I was ready to open the door and escape.

"I'll ask you again, how much money have you withdrawn from that account?"

"I… I… You didn't put your pay in it?—" I was really stuttering now.

"*I'm asking you for the last time, how much money did you withdraw from that account?*" Maya was really yelling and she was wearing an ugly mocking expression. I looked back at her face, thinking to myself, *How could I have ever loved such a horrible woman?* I went on thinking, ignoring the situation I was in. After a moment of silence I answered, "I don't know. Excuse me—"

I walked slowly to the other side of the kitchen toward the door leading to the garage. My oldest daughter, Ally, suddenly ran toward me and I was surprised to see the look on her face. I had never before seen this kind of expression on my child's face and I realized that my daughter had been dragged into this circle of intimidation. She'd realized how powerless I was compared to her mother and her grandmother and she didn't want to be excluded, or perhaps as a small child she had to join in and show her alliance with whomever she thought was the strongest. At that moment I knew it was the beginning of a new scenario. I wasn't only losing my manipulative wife but I was also going to lose my daughters.

"Answer the question!" Ally yelled at me and I just stared at her in disbelief. *Is this the daughter I raised*, I wondered, and felt a sudden urge to sing the song from the play we had seen just one year ago, *Fiddler on the Roof*. I started humming quietly and all were looking at me as though I was going mad.

"Is this the little girl I carried?"
"Is this the little girl at play?"

I paused for a second and looked at my daughter. She was obviously confused and looked at her mother as if asking for confirmation to go ahead. Maya just stood there silently with an artificial expression of disbelief on her face.

> *"I don't remember her growing older*
> *When did she?*
> *Sunrise, sunset*
> *Sunrise, sunset*
> *Swiftly flow the days*
> *Seedlings turn overnight to sunflowers*
> *Blossoming even as we gaze."*

I continued humming and looking at the walls, because I couldn't look at their hate-filled faces. Then I saw my little daughter, Anika, staring at me with a look of appreciation and respect, and I realized that she was the only one trying to understand the words of the song I was humming. I looked at her little face and she smiled at me. She understood my pain and I realized that she was the only one who really cared about what was happening to me, her father.

"How much money did you withdraw from that account?" Maya yelled again, bringing everyone's attention back to her.

"I didn't take anything," I answered faintly. Maya looked straight into my eyes, and it was one of the rare moments in our relationship when she could hold my stare. I realized she wasn't dealing with me on a human-to-human level, it was more like evil angry animal to helpless human being. She was in control and had all the power and she knew it. It showed in her contempt for me.

"I'm going to the bank now!" Maya said and headed towards me. I noticed my daughter was also storming towards me. Maya put her hand on my daughter's shoulder and gave her a push forward, encouraging her to do what she had intended — push me.

"Stop it, Ally!" I said, upset and hurt.

"How much money did you withdraw from the account?" I heard Maya asking again, assuming that our daughter's imitation of her mother would deliver a different answer from me.

"She's imitating you. You know why she's angry... you know why she's angry," I heard myself responding.

Maya stepped forward and her face was just inches away from mine.

"Come on, hit me, hit me," I goaded her. "It's what you want to do. Your *sweet* old mother tried it yesterday. I ran away. What? Do you think that this is normal adult activity to show our children?" I paused for a second, hoping to get some understanding response; but instead Maya was getting physically closer to me while Ally, realizing the grave situation her father was in, was pulling back.

"Ally...Ally!" I heard Anika yell. She was always protective of me and was trying to defend me.

"You're all crazy!" Ally screamed and I was astonished by her response, considering that she was only 4 years old.

"You bounced a check again!" Maya was getting really angry, or was it only part of her show? I wasn't sure that what was happening was real.

"I'm going to *bury* you, you know!" Maya's screechy voice seemed to thunder near my ears. *Yes, it is real,* I thought. "Okay, bury me!" I answered.

"I'm going to fucking bury you now!"

"Maya, you're yelling too close to my ears. You can make me deaf but not dead from your yelling. I'm going to go now."

"Where are you going?"

Then I saw Maya's mother approaching me and I knew she was party to this whole show. She didn't care that her grandchildren were there; she didn't care about anything involving me. She wanted her daughter to be divorced and she joined forces with her to achieve this objective. She wanted history to repeat itself — she was divorced and had probably orchestrated similar events with her husband over 25 years ago.

I heard the mastermind's voice with its very pronounced accent yelling from behind me, "Okay, I'll call police!"

"So, call the police," I said and I tried to exit through the garage door.

"Call the police!"

"I'll call," I heard Maya's voice faintly responding. Maya picked up the phone and dialed the Marlboro police.

"I need assistance at 17 Memory Road. My husband is crazy and he's trying to hurt my daughter and me... he's acting violently!"

"Really?" I asked with great irony. I just stood there next to the garage door. I couldn't move, I couldn't think, I couldn't say anything. I was just standing there hoping the garage door would open by itself so I could get out of this nightmare.

The police came within several minutes and three cruisers were assigned to my address. I looked around and the only faces I could focus on were the faces of my two little innocent girls, who probably couldn't believe what was happening.

Suddenly I was brought back to the present when I heard a Russian accent. Looking up, I saw Ingrid in the witness seat discussing something with the court's interpreter.

INTERPRETER: "The witness wants to apologize for the fact that she doesn't speak English."
JUDGE: "Not at all. It's perfectly all right. This country is made up of people who come from other countries so that's perfectly fine. We have a translator. Thank you for coming. What's your sister's name?
MAYA: "Ilona Kissall."
JUDGE: "Ms. Kissall, why don't you place your bag down, and make your way up to the witness box. As you arrive, please place your papers down. Place your left hand on the Bible, and raise your right hand. Please state your name and spell your last name."
ILONA: "Ilona Kissall. K-i-s-s-a-l-l."
JUDGE: "Thank you very much. Please be seated. Now, you're the sister of the plaintiff, is that correct? "
ILONA: "Yes."
JUDGE: "And it is my understanding that a phone call was placed to the former marital residence of the parties."
ILONA: "Correct."
JUDGE: "On or about November 3rd, November 4th, do you remember which day it was?"
ILONA: "No, not really."
JUDGE: "Okay."
ILONA: "The children were out of school, on holiday."
JUDGE: "In any event, so do you remember what time the phone call was placed to the residence?"
ILONA: "It was morning."
JUDGE: "And the children were home?"
ILONA: "Yes."
JUDGE: "So when you answered the phone, did you recognize the voice at the other end?"
ILONA: "Yes, I did."

JUDGE: "And whose voice was it?"
ILONA: "My ex-brother-in-law, David."
JUDGE: "The defendant who is seated here in Judge Killmen's court?"
ILONA: "Yes."
JUDGE: "And did he identify himself or did you simply recognize his voice?"
ILONA: "He identified himself to me, actually."
JUDGE: "And what did he say? What can you recall him saying?"
ILONA: "He said that my bitch sister deserves to die and he's going to kill her one day."

That statement didn't seem real and it was probably taken from some low-grade horror movie, but again Judge Killmen and my lawyer allowed it into the court record.

JUDGE: "Do you remember him saying anything else?"
ILONA: "No, I hung up the phone. However, I didn't know at that time that my niece had picked up the phone upstairs. And then he said to her that something bad would happen to all of us if they would not live with him. And we just heard her screaming upstairs. I ran upstairs. She was calling 911. Then police came. Also, she was advised by 911 to call DYFS."
JUDGE: "So Ally was screaming and she called 911?"
ILONA: "Yeah, and I was there."
JUDGE: "Now, before this phone call, had the defendant ever made any other threats about your sister to you?"
ILONA: "Yes, many times. It's ongoing for sure, forever actually, since the beginning of their relationship. Many times when they were quarreling, he would like call her names, always threatening. He threatened the whole family while the divorce was going on.

"He, well, I'm living in Latvia right now where I'm working and he would call to Latvia and he would call my father in Ukraine. He would call my aunts in Ukraine and threaten them. He just threatens everybody and says that something bad is going to happen to me, something bad is going to happen to my sister. She doesn't deserve to live. She's a prostitute. She doesn't deserve to live. She's a prostitute. She's a bitch. She's this and that and something else. And it's just never stopping."

That was another blatant lie that the judge ignored. How could I call anyone in Ukraine and speak Russian or Ukrainian? What language could I speak with Maya's family? I do not know anyone of their family members, as they do not have any family that keep in touch with them.

JUDGE: "Are you afraid for your sister?"
ILONA: "Yes, I am."
JUDGE: "You believe she's in danger?"
ILONA: "Yes, I do. I ask her to please ask someone to walk her to the car because she works in a hospital and she comes home late. Also, I ask police to come home and actually wait when she comes home."
JUDGE: "Okay."
ILONA: "It's very hard to predict what this man is going to do next."
JUDGE: "All right, Todd Prone, do you have any questions?"
TODD: "Yes, Your Honor."
TODD: "You testified that David threatened you or your sister?"
ILONA: "Both of us."
TODD: "That wasn't your testimony."
ILONA: "Yeah, that's what I said. He called to Latvia where I live right now."
TODD: "Did he threaten you on that date, did he threaten you or did he threaten Maya?"
ILONA: "No, he didn't threaten me on that date. He threatened my sister and he said to my niece that something bad is going to happen –"
TODD: "Okay. So he threatened your sister on that date. Now, in the complaint for the temporary restraining order, it's not stated that he threatened to kill anybody. You didn't tell the police that he threatened to kill anybody."
ILONA: "Yes, I did. I'm not quite sure what was written on that report. "

TODD: "So it's your testimony that the police haven't included in the report."

ILONA: "I don't know. That's what was said to the police."

JUDGE: "The temporary restraining order wasn't prepared by the police. It was prepared here at Judge Killmen's court."

ILONA: "And as a matter of fact, the police are very aware of the fact that David is calling everybody and stalking my sister constantly. Mr. Fox from the police said that he talked to David a few times."

TODD: "Objection. *Todd's voice was faint and quivering. The judge just ignored him and continued the show.*

ILONA: "Because he was –"

JUDGE: "Ms. Kissall, no question is pending."

ILONA: "I'm sorry."

JUDGE: "Next question."

TODD: "Nothing further, Your Honor."

JUDGE: "All right. Thank you. You can step down. You can sit next to your mother and remain in Judge Killmen's room. Thank you very much. All right, the plaintiff rests at this point. Todd Prone."

TODD: "I would like to call David, Your Honor, to the stand."

JUDGE: "Okay. He can remain there if he's more comfortable since the plaintiff remained there."

TODD: "Do you feel more comfortable sitting there?"

DAVID: "Yes."

JUDGE: "Okay, he has all his papers there."

TODD: "All right. David, how long were you and Maya married?"

DAVID: "We were married about ten years. Eight and a half years of that she was in a legal proceeding called deportation."

From the angle of my eye I saw Judge Killmen staring at me with a look of dismay. She didn't like my response, bringing up the deportation issue, which would make Maya look bad. Yes, an immigrant who not only was in the country illegally, but who had lied about her status as a refugee to get into the country in the first place. Judge Killmen must have been fooled by the crocodile tears forming in her mother's eyes as she gave her testimony, with her dramatic motion of pulling out a handkerchief to catch the tears as they ran down her cheeks. That woman deserved an academy award! They all do. I could easily envision the three women going over their stories about the threatening' phone calls, the stalking, the drive-by shouting, how they all needed to keep on the same desperate track. I wonder if the tears were planned as well. But was I good enough at acting to hold down my outrage under questioning? I felt like my limbs were those of a puppet, being played with by children. Nothing was moving right, my body or my thoughts.

TODD: "Okay. Now, David, you've been involved in divorce proceedings, correct?"

DAVID: "Yes."

TODD: "How long have you been involved in these divorce proceedings?"

DAVID: "Just from January of this year. I was served the divorce papers just before leaving the house, in mid-January. I know that it states in the police report that it was filed in December but I was served in late January."

TODD: "And because certain things have happened with your children, your custody with your children, what has happened?"

DAVID: "There was a decision here, a civil restraining order that I agreed to leave the marital home and get normal scheduled visitations, which I went forward with because it entitled me to see my children regularly. I left the marital home and hoped the civil restraining order would help bring the end of this marriage in an orderly way."

JUDGE: "It has been marked P-1, that's what P—1 is."

TODD: "P—1, Your Honor, thank you. "

JUDGE: "Do you need to see it, Todd Prone?"

TODD: "No, it's okay, Your Honor, I have a copy."

DAVID: "I signed this agreement and even though this divorce was a surprise for me, I was determined to abide by this restraining order. I followed it to the word. I was expecting to get my visitation rights, which were blocked. "

TODD: "All right, so you were afforded visitation."

DAVID: "I was afforded visitation but it was blocked for different reasons."

TODD: "What do you mean by it was blocked for different reasons?"

DAVID: At the beginning the children were sick, it started that way; the children were sick. They didn't feel well. They had plans. They had this and they had that. Toward the end of March the reasons changed and it turned out that my older child didn't want to see me at all."

TODD: "Did you have scheduled visitation?"

DAVID: "Yes."

TODD: "And would you show up at the house for visitation?"

DAVID: "Yes."

TODD: "Okay. And when you would show up at the house for visitation, would the children come out?"

DAVID: "At the beginning, yes, for the first several visits. Then after that, I would just go home because nobody opened the door."

TODD: "So in the interim, you had the visitation rights that you were supposed to be getting, but you weren't actually able to realize your rights, and what happened after that?"

DAVID: "In May, my lawyer advised me to file a motion to restate visitation and I said I didn't want to go for the legal course, since there would be more expenses for me and for my spouse."

TODD: "Just as an aside, you're representing yourself in the divorce, correct?"

DAVID: "Yes."

TODD: "Okay. So you're a pro-se litigant and you don't have an attorney for that, correct?"

DAVID: "That's right. So I didn't file the motion. I said that I would like to negotiate visitation rights as agreeable and have the divorce end on good terms. I submitted a letter to Maya in February saying that we're both parents of the same children, and the divorce should be conducted in a way that won't damage our children. It was a pathetic letter, saying I want to have less legal intervention and asking to let's have the kids visitation back to normal, have the divorce amicably, and I'll agree with all the terms of divorce. After this letter, all hell broke out. In May I received an emergency motion filed against me, declaring me insane and dangerous to my children, on the fact that I for seven years had been an Air Force officer and a soldier. And further because I wrote that manuscript in a therapy session six months before."

TODD: "Let's talk about the manuscript for a second. Now, you wrote this manuscript. Are you an author?"

DAVID: "I'm an author part-time. It's not my claim to fame, but I'm an author and about 100,000 readers per year read my articles."

TODD: "And what kind of articles do you write?"

DAVID: "Mostly political essays and current affairs essays."

TODD: "And these are published articles, correct?"

DAVID: "Yes."

TODD: "Okay. And how do you use your writing? Why do you write?"

DAVID: "Most of the articles I write are with an objective. I get an idea, a way to improve things. For example, I wrote an article about hormones that people inject cows with, which can affect the health of human beings who eat the meat or drink cow's milk."

TODD: "' Do you use writing to relax?"

DAVID: "Yes."

TODD: "Do you use writing as a cathartic experience to deal with your life?"

DAVID: "Yes."

TODD: "So this manuscript that was written, who suggested that you write the manuscript?"

DAVID: "Ms. Mally, the therapist who specializes in September 11th victims who are going through a personal crisis."

TODD: "Can you say that again? I'm sorry."

DAVID: "Ms. Mally is a therapist who was referred to me by some friends. She specializes in helping September 11th victims who were in that area at the time the buildings went down, and who are going through a personal crisis."

TODD: "Okay. So you wrote the manuscript upon her suggestion?"

DAVID: "Her encouragement."

TODD: "After you wrote the manuscript, describe the course of events that followed."

DAVID: "I wrote the manuscript in November, after the first session with Ms. Mally, and I told Ms. Mally about the manuscript. I told her that it is going to be dramatic. I'm choosing a dramatic end because it's symbolic, it's a metaphor, a way to reconcile the fact my wife doesn't love me, my children are lost to me, the horror of September 11th. It was a private communication between my therapist and me. I thought I was protected by psychologist-client confidentiality, similar to attorney-client privilege. I never thought I'll be in any situation where this manuscript would be used outside of a therapy session, especially by somebody who is a psychologist."

TODD: "Okay. So you used this manuscript as a way to deal with the breaking up of your marriage?"

DAVID: "Yes."

TODD: "Okay. And was this manuscript ever used against you subsequently?"

DAVID: "Many times."

TODD: "Okay. And what happened as a result of this manuscript?"

DAVID: "In November, Maya found the manuscript on my computer. And when she came to meet Ms. Mally in one of the sessions I had, she was very annoyed at the way she was portrayed in this manuscript. Ms. Mally wrote the letter to Judge Irish in July about this issue, stating that Maya came to the session, describing her behavior, and that I was basically describing an abusive relationship at the hands of an abusive woman."

TODD: "But she wrote a letter to Judge Irish explaining why you wrote this manuscript."

DAVID: "Yes."

TODD: "And it was her opinion at that time that it was therapeutic."

DAVID: "Yes."

TODD: "Keep going with your story."

DAVID: "And the title of the manuscript is 'Psychologists with no God.'"

TODD: "I'm sorry to interrupt. Let's talk about what happened as a result of this manuscript."

DAVID: "Generally, suddenly I was told by police that there's a Temporary Restraining Order pending, that I better prepare to leave the house before I get kicked out. I left the house on January 26th basically only with a suitcase."

TODD: "Okay. And you moved out."

DAVID: "I moved to an apartment in Aberdeen."

TODD: "How many miles away is that from your former residence?"

DAVID: "It's about twenty miles."

JUDGE: "You still live at that same place?"

DAVID: "Yes."

JUDGE: "Twenty miles away?"

DAVID: "Twenty miles away and next to a train station. I hardly use my car as I commute to New York City and just walk to the station."

JUDGE: "Okay. What color car do you have?"

DAVID: "It's a white car, but I didn't drive that car for about two months after I moved out.

I put about sixty miles on it in two months, 40 miles of which were to travel to the courthouse."

TODD: "David, what happened with your custody situation after that manuscript was written?"

DAVID: "By February I was out of the house. We came to Judge Killmen's court here and we signed a civil order that I believed would be followed by both parties. I tried to do my part. I just came for visitation and paid support and alimony even though she earns more than I do. I followed all orders, whatever was needed specifically according to Judge Irish's order of April this year."

TODD: "Were your visitation rights ever terminated or were they ever altered because of this?"

DAVID: "There was a motion filed in April to have supervised visitations, but that motion was denied."

TODD: "Okay."

DAVID: "However, I didn't get visitation, normal visitation until now."

TODD: "But wasn't there, as part of Judge Killmen's order, the stipulation that you were only allowed to see your children under certain circumstances, is that correct?"

DAVID: "Until the end of May, though I was allowed to see them unsupervised, there were no visitations. I used to go to see them, but nobody would answer the door, and police was called to knock on the door as I had to follow the civil order."

TODD: "And then how about after May? What happened after May?"

DAVID: "After May, Maya filed an emergency motion with her lawyer, Bettina Mussolini, to show that I'm insane and dangerous. She brought up my military service and my writing of six months before, written in therapy, as the basis for a motion to stop visitation."

TODD: "Was that motion granted?"

DAVID: "Yes."

TODD: "So the motion was granted and what were the terms of Judge Irish's orders?"

DAVID: "Judge Irish requested a psychological report or a risk assessment."

TODD: "Did you get one?"

DAVID: "I submitted a detailed report with my psychological profile which said that I'm just a 'nice very normal guy', and a custody report that didn't find anything bad about me. Also. Ms. Mally sent a letter to Judge Irish stating that Maya had come to her in November last year, and adding that she didn't find anything worthy of concern based on the manuscript."

TODD: "Well, let me ask you this. Did you comply with all of Judge Irish's orders?"

DAVID: "I did."

TODD: "Every single one?"

DAVID: "Every single one, including a risk assessment that again found that nothing was wrong with me, and a custody evaluation which I went to, that found nothing was wrong. I have a copy here of both the Risk Assessment and the Custody Evaluation. It was surprising that Maya brought up this hearing just six days before I was hoping to finally be allowed to see my children."

TODD: "We'll get to that, David. So as you were going through this process, you were looking forward to seeing your children again, correct?"

DAVID: Yes, very much so. I do not plan to fall within the group of 40% of American men who do not see their children ever again after divorce, because of the legal costs and the heavy premiums needed to maintain relationship with their children. I had paid nearly $80,000 in legal fees to restore visitations and then this issue was brought up by Maya."

TODD: "David, you're representing yourself in this matter, as we've already discussed. And you knew that in representing yourself, you were going to have to file certain papers with Judge Irish, correct?"

DAVID: "Yes. I was representing myself but I had help from two friends as I had run out of funds and I cannot afford to continue legal representation in the family court, where wrangling between lawyers just increased my bills. There was a lot of wrangling in this case, as both the opposing lawyer and my lawyer noticed we both had some money in savings, and they easily helped us deplete our savings."

TODD: "But your pleadings, your answers, your motions, you prepared them yourself, correct?

DAVID: "I prepared them myself, yes."

TODD: "David, do you recognize these documents, this grouping of documents here?"

DAVID: "These are all motions. They were prepared in the last two months."

TODD: "In the last two months, during a time when you've been trying to get your custody and visitation back, correct?"

DAVID: It actually took me six months to prepare everything, all the exhibits and the risk assessment; I requested that Judge Irish look into Maya's secret bank accounts, and also define my visitation and phone rights. I requested e-mail rights for my children that were blocked from May. I also requested enforcement for the disposal of our marital home which was ordered by Judge Irish in August and which my spouse chooses not to follow as she lives there without paying the mortgage as ordered by Judge Irish. "

TODD: "It has taken you months to prepare this paperwork to get to see your children again, correct?"

DAVID: "Two months for the paperwork, four months for the exhibits, six months total. "

TODD: "So after months and months of work, putting these pleadings, these motions, and your exhibits together in an attempt to get custody of your children, on the same day you go to court, allegedly on November 4th, and file your final paperwork, your final pleading with Judge Irish after all this hard work, correct?"

DAVID: "Yes, that's correct."

TODD: "At what time did you do that?"

DAVID: "Eight-thirty in the morning. At nine o'clock I was in Bettina Mussolini's office and served the papers. At 9:40 a.m. I was in the train station going to New York City. At eleven in the morning I was in New York City."

TODD: "And you were at work for the rest of the day."

DAVID: "Yes, I have my time sheets with me."

TODD: "David, did you call your wife's house on that day?"

DAVID: "I'm not crazy. I mean, I have six months of work here done in order to restore my relations with my children. I'm not stupid to do something like that. It just doesn't make sense. I don't have any motives to destroy my future with my children. "

TODD: "Just to be clear, all of these motions were set to be heard before Judge Irish on November 14th."

DAVID: "November 13th."

TODD: "Just seven days before this Temporary Restraining Order was issued, correct?"
DAVID: "Yes."
TODD: "And let me ask you. What would happen with Judge Irish if he knew that you contacted your wife or your wife's family and threatened them?"
DAVID: "Judge Irish would disregard those motions."
TODD: "And your six months worth of work—"
DAVID: "Would go down the drain."
TODD: "Nothing further, Your Honor."

Now Judge Killer-of-men took over the examination, her tone hostile as she questioned me again about my wife's accusations. Her body language seemed to state she didn't like me one bit. I was nervous and defensive, but showed no fear. I defended myself as well as I could against all the lies, but with so many of them, could the judge wade through the mire?

JUDGE: "Is it true that you've driven past her approximately five times and yelled out to her things such as "I'll kill you, you Russian prostitute?"
DAVID: "Your honor, I would never say such things, or harm my family in this way. One of the things that was mentioned earlier was the fact that I served in the Air Force for seven years. I did my duty and I don't believe in violence at home. I didn't grow up in an abusive household. I know that had my family ever found that I had raised a hand on or abused a woman, or a child, they would sever any relationship with me.

"Why would I drive by the house and commit stupid or violent acts, screaming or threatening anyone? What language was I using to yell at Maya's family? Her mother stated that I drove next to the house calling out to her, but she says she only understands Russian. How could she or Maya's father understand what I'm saying on the phone or in person? I don't speak Russian! So, it would be impossible for them to understand anything I said to them."

JUDGE: "Is it true that you called her dentist to ask when her next appointment was?"

DAVID: "I didn't call the dentist to ask about her next appointment, I called to verify that my wife was at his office because she said she was there when she should have been at an appointment with my children. We had a reunification therapy session ordered by Judge Irish through Mr. Muller.

"My parents had just come from overseas, flying 11 hours to see their grandchildren. There was a one-hour visitation set up so my parents could see the. Maya showed up 55 minutes late. That meant there were only five minutes left for visitation and only my oldest daughter was there.

"Again, Maya claimed she was at the dentist's office, so I called the dentist trying to find her. He said he couldn't give me that information, so I just said 'okay' and hung up."

I sat staring at the ceiling and my mind flashed back to three months ago and the much-anticipated visit by my parents. They were going to visit for a week. Their happiness was mixed with a touch of dread because they were afraid they might not be able to see their grandchildren on this visit, and might not be allowed to see them ever again.

They knew that Maya wanted me to disappear from her life and that meant disappearing from our children's lives as well. I wouldn't let that happen. I was making every possible effort to restore my relationship with my children while Maya did her best to end it.

Mr. Muller organized a visitation with my parents and they were excited to finally get to see their grandchildren. We spent the Sunday in the mall and bought several gifts for the children. I was surprised to see my father so excited.

We waited in Mr. Muller's office until 5:55 p.m. Just before the end of the session, Maya showed up with Ally. For some reason, Anika wasn't with her. My mother tried to hug Ally, but Ally backed away. Mr. Muller witnessed this, but didn't do anything to help.

We all left the room without saying a word to each other. My father was shocked and my mother was trying to hold back tears. At the last second, my mother ran after Ally and tried to hug her again. Maya approached my mother and warned her harshly, "Get away from my child!" My mother's face was filled with anguish and sadness as she heard Maya's cruel words and saw the hatred in her eyes.

After a few seconds, as though she woke up from a dream, she yelled back, "She's also my son's daughter!"

Maya just glared at her, with hatred emanating from every pore.

The Judge's voice brought me back to her courtroom.

JUDGE: "Is it true that you have called her work, contrary to this consent order for civil restraints filed February 22nd marked P—1?"

DAVID: "No, Your Honor. I work in the Stock Exchange. Every call is monitored—"

JUDGE: "Is it true that you've attempted to call the house?"

DAVID: "No, Your Honor."

JUDGE: "Is it true that you actually got through to the house and spoke to the plaintiff's mother?"

DAVID: "No, Your Honor. The police, the Marlboro police, would be there; just see the reports. I also do not speak Russian."

TODD: "Yes or no?"

DAVID: "No, Your Honor."

JUDGE: "And since January of this year, how many times have you been contacted by the Marlboro police?"

DAVID: "About 20 times."

JUDGE: "Were you contacted on or about November 3rd or November 4th?"

DAVID: "No. They stopped contacting me after August because they got the picture that this constant filing of reports had no basis in truth."

JUDGE: "Have you heard from the Division of Youth and Family Services?"

DAVID: "Yes."

JUDGE: "When did they contact you?"

DAVID: "They came to my house several times and then dismissed all complaints. I don't understand how my spouse claimed she didn't get the letter of dismissal. All complaints were dismissed."

TODD: "Your Honor, can I mark this as a defense exhibit?"

JUDGE: "Why don't we mark that D—2?"

TODD: "This is a letter from DYFS terminating the investigation."

JUDGE: "Okay, can you just mark that?"

TODD: "This is a letter dated November 18th from the Department of Children and Family, Division of Youth and Family Services. It says, 'Dear David, New Jersey law requires the Division of Youth and Family Services to investigate all allegations of child abuse and neglect. On 11/7, the Division northern Monmouth local office received an allegation that Ally Tal had been neglected.

"The Division conducted its required investigation and determined that the allegation was unfounded. Therefore, the Division won't keep a record of the investigation results on its central registry. The Division won't be providing further service to your family. Current law provides that this information may not be disclosed by anyone, including yourself.' We request that this letter be moved into evidence."

JUDGE: "I'll move that letter into evidence. It's an original letter from that entity. So, David, you're telling me that the plaintiff is lying when she says that you violated the civil restraining order?"

DAVID: "She's lying, yes."

JUDGE: "Is it true that you followed her after the economic mediation in October of this year?"

DAVID: "It's not true."

JUDGE: "Is it true that you cut her off on Route 9 on July 14th?"

DAVID: "It's not true. I was in Freehold with Dr. Psylie at that time."

TODD: "Your Honor, if I may. Can I mark this as defense Exhibit 3?"

JUDGE: "What's that?"

TODD: "This is a bill from Dr. Psylie that shows that the defendant was actually in three separate 45-minute therapy sessions on July 14th.

David, you had just finished a therapy session, correct, a court ordered therapy session?"

DAVID: "No, it was a custody evaluation. According to what the plaintiff says, she took the children home and then she drove somewhere on Route 9. When she filed her report, she didn't even mention to the police that it was me following her.

"I don't understand where all these allegations are coming from. There's a pack of police reports by which I can substantiate my alibi and my whereabouts for each of these allegations. The dates for some of the reports were times when I was overseas or on vacation.

"For example, there was a police report filed on September 3rd saying that I burglarized the house. I was in Canada on that date. The police never saw me in the vicinity of the home nor did anyone else, but they were obligated to take a report."

TODD: "Nothing further, Your Honor."

JUDGE: "So, David, in your opinion, the plaintiff is here seeking a restraining order simply to get a leg up in the custody battle?"

DAVID: "Not only custody. There are other issues that were supposed to be decided on November 13th. The immigration followed by citizenship issue is also relevant but couldn't be presented here. She cannot get her citizenship unless this hearing goes in her favor. Maya's accusations were basically meant to preempt, in my opinion, Judge Irish's decision, because Judge Irish has all the documentation and exhibits to make a decision about what's good for my children. I wouldn't do what was alleged. I have always respected the law, and this is an insult to truth and justice."

JUDGE: "Okay. When was the last time you spoke to Ingrid Getall, the plaintiff's mother?"

DAVID: "The last time I saw her was on September 3rd when we met in a session with the child therapist. Maya showed up 55 minutes late. I didn't speak to her that day."

JUDGE: "When was the last time you spoke to Ilona Kissall?"

DAVID: "I haven't seen her since last year. It's been over a year since I've seen or spoken to her."

JUDGE: "It appears from the police report that has been marked P—2, that you called your marital home on Nov. 3rd."

DAVID: "On November 3rd I was at work. I work for the Stock Exchange. Every phone call is monitored, so it's not possible—"

JUDGE: "Do you have a cell phone?"

DAVID: "Yes. I have a cell phone record and I have my house phone records. There were no phone calls made by me to any of my family members during that time."

JUDGE: "So your cell phone records indicate that you made no outgoing phone calls?"

TODD: "Your Honor, I have the cell phone records for the date in question. They indicate that he didn't make any calls to New Jersey. May I mark these as a defense exhibit?"

JUDGE: "Sure. So being marked, are his cell phone records from November 3rd? Is November 4th also included?"

TODD: "November 4th also is included, Your Honor."

JUDGE: "What's the house phone number?"

MAYA: "732-555-1212. New York City has many public phones or you can borrow somebody's phone. It doesn't have to be your own."

DAVID: "Definitely, they are not private and the phone numbers should be displayed on your caller ID or your phone record. You should have a record and you didn't present one."

JUDGE: "According to this cell phone record, you made only one phone call on November 3rd and two phone calls on November 4th."

DAVID: "On November 3rd I was with my friend, Mr. Vince Urbank, who was helping me to finalize the last answer for Judge Irish. The November 4th *calls were ones I made to my family in Canada*"

MAYA: "So maybe you used Vince's phone then?"

TODD: "Objection! Your Honor, may I have this marked? This is his home phone record from the same dates."

JUDGE: "We'll make that D—5. And you say the call came to your house's phone, Maya?"

MAYA: "Yes."

TODD: "I believe this is the Comcast bill for the same dates."

JUDGE: "From these bills marked D—5 it doesn't appear that there were any phone calls placed to that number. So you're saying on November 3rd and November 4th, you were at work both days?"

DAVID: "Yes, Your Honor."

TODD: "In the late morning hours?"

DAVID: "On Wednesday, November 4th, I showed up late at work, about 10:30 or eleven o'clock, because I was at court filing the motion for Judge Irish's hearing."

JUDGE: "Okay. Maya, do you have any questions of David?"

MAYA: "Yes, Your Honor. The DYFS letters you received, David, said that they received an allegation on November 7th, but it wasn't pertaining to November 3rd or November 4th. Usually when DYFS gets an allegation, they have to send someone out within 24 hours. I know the system. "

DAVID: "It's a lie, Maya."

MAYA: "In our case, DYFS was involved many times. So I don't know why I haven't received anything from DYFS yet."

TODD: "Your Honor, is this a question or this an accusation?"

MAYA: "No, this is clarification."

JUDGE: "Ask it in the form of a question is what he's saying."

MAYA: "In that DYFS letter that you received, David, was it regarding the incident that took place on November 3rd?"

DAVID: "They said that they already knew the situation. Every allegation has to go by a specific person that they, by law, are supposed to investigate every allegation. I don't know if there is any letter here about November 3rd. There were three letters submitted by DYFS. Every imaginary allegation was dismissed. They came to interview me several times and were surprised to know that I haven't seen my children for many months, thus they didn't understand why DYFS was called."

TODD: "Your Honor, we're alleging that this letter we provided was the summation of the DYFS investigation on this case."

MAYA: "Is it true that Mr. Muller advised Judge Irish that you had threatened him?"

DAVID: "No. Mr. Muller was appointed as our reunification therapist."

JUDGE: "I really don't want to hear the whole long story. I just want to know if it is true that Mr. Muller advised Judge Irish that you had threatened him?"

DAVID: "Yes, I threatened him with a lawsuit because of his ineffective treatments and the way he was handling my children. Also because he took this case without having any experience with reunification sessions involving children who have signs of Parental Alienation. Plus, he was affiliated with my spouse's counsel's law office. He was performing services for the opposing counsel while billing me. I felt that was a conflict of interest."

JUDGE: "Would you like to ask more questions of David, Maya?"

MAYA: "Yes, please."

JUDGE KILLMEN: "Okay, next question."

MAYA: "Is it true, David, that it was Judge Irish who actually stopped your visitations, not me?"

DAVID: "It was your motion. The Judge made a decision based on evidence. You submitted evidence, the manuscript you stole knowing it was used in therapy sessions. You used it to humiliate me. In my opinion, Judge Irish thought that because you're a psychologist everything you said was believable. You perjured yourself repeatedly in front of Judge Irish and now in this court, which is feeling more like an inquisition than a court proceeding to me."

TODD: "Okay, let's leave your opinions out of it."

DAVID: "That's the reason I prepared everything for Judge Irish. I was looking forward to that date so justice would prevail and my children would have the father the plaintiff tried so hard to remove from their lives."

MAYA: "Did you come to my workplace at the prison on January 15? You know there are all kinds of cameras and everything else there.

DAVID: "Until I was served divorce papers in mid-January, I didn't know you wanted a divorce. I thought you were going just through some sort of crisis. I came to your work once with a dozen roses. I told the guard that I was your husband and asked him to let you know I was waiting. You work in a jail, it's not like I can just wander in and stalk you like you're trying to suggest. Had I really been stalking you, I wouldn't be standing here today because the prison guards would've taken me down."

MAYA: "Did you cut me off on Route 9?"

DAVID: "You know very well I *did not*, and I don't lie."

MAYA: "I know otherwise, David."

TODD: "Your Honor, she's both testifying and asking questions."

JUDGE: "All right, let's stick to questions."

MAYA: "David, did you stop the payment to Dr. Psylie because she didn't write what you expected her to write about you?"

DAVID: "Only the last bill was paid late."

MAYA: "It was?"

DAVID: "I paid all the bills in full."

JUDGE: "Any other questions? I realize there's a legitimate issue and I appreciate that. I think I've heard enough testimony to get a sense of things. I'm ready to decide the case"

We all got up when the court officer yelled, "All rise!" Judge Killmen got up and went to her chambers, but not before exchanging a glance with me. It wasn't a good sign. I sat awaiting my fate as memories took me back to other times.

CHAPTER ELEVEN

The Terror

On September 11, 2001, I woke up early and took a look at the outside world. This had been my habit for years. It was my way of figuring out how to dress for the day and if I should take an umbrella. I could see that it was going to be a beautiful day, with not a cloud in the sky. I headed to the shower with my spirits high.

I showered, shaved and chose my black suit, one of my white dress shirts and my red flowery tie as the outfit of the day. I was scheduled to meet with my boss later on and wanted to look sharp.

I had no way of knowing that I would be witness to the greatest terrorist act of mankind's history on that day. I left for work relatively early and took the ferry to my office on Wall Street. My office was on the 16th floor in a crummy-looking grey building. It wasn't much better on the inside with it's white and a dull grey walls — it looked more like a government building than a financial institution.

I took the elevator to the 16th floor, got my coffee and bagel and headed to my office. I thought I could relax a bit before my hectic schedule kicked in. I was feeling relaxed and content. I logged into my workspace on the computer, and as the login welcome screen appeared the screen blinked for a second. I had seen this happen before when there was a power surge at home, but I'd never had it happen in the corporate environment. Immediately after that happened, the lights flickered.

I got up from my chair, worried about was happening with the electrical system on my floor. I walked briskly towards the window, wondering, *Has the weather changed?* I looked out my window and I saw lots of pieces of paper flying around in the air. "Hooligans!" I yelled thinking someone was littering on a monstrous scale.

I heard my phone ringing and casually wondered who would be calling me so early. When I picked it up, I heard my brother's voice. He wasn't talking, though, he was screaming frantically into the phone. He was saying that an airplane had crashed into the World Trade center and the building was on fire. He was panicking because he thought the building was going to collapse.

"No, the towers won't collapse," I assured him. "They're designed to withstand that sort of thing"

"Don't get close to the towers. You need to stay away. Promise me you won't come here!" he begged before ending the phone call.

I hung up the phone and was ready to walk down Wall Street to see exactly what was going on. Before I could leave my office, my brother called again and frantically asked me to go home as soon as possible. My brother knew me well, and realized I would find it hard to resist helping anyone who needed it after this tragedy. After all I was once an Air Force officer.

One minute later he called me again and pleaded with me to go home. I took me several more minutes to think over my brother's pleas, and then I decided to go outside and see what was happening. I walked down Wall Street and passed Trinity Church. I was surprised to see the gates of the church were closed and wondered why.

I continued my walk toward the towers — I was one of the few going that direction. A police officer looked at me for a second and I waved my office badge to him and continued walking. When I reached Thames Street, I got a full view of the towers and heard faint sounds of buckling metal.

I'd seen evil before, and the big gaping hole in tower was indeed evil. "It was for sure an airplane," I said to myself as I continued walking. I was thinking about the terrible way the people inside the doomed airplane and ruined building died.

I stood for a moment next to a man holding a camera heard him saying, "People are jumping from the building." He gasped and then screamed as he pointed toward the top of the tower, "Another one is jumping!" The smoke was billowing from the towers and I saw one small dot falling from one of the windows. I realized it was a person had escaped one mode of death only to replace it with another that was just as horrific.

I was standing there trying to decide what to do, when I realized that something worse was going to happen. I heard a noise that sounded like rolling thunder with underlying sounds of twisted metal screaming and I instinctively turned around and ran as quickly as I could. While passing Trinity Church on my right, I glanced behind it and I saw the top of the tower starting to collapse.

For a second, the story from the Bible about Lot's wife came to my mind, and I had the irrational thought that if I stood there I would be frozen and turned into salt. It wasn't an appropriate thing to think in that moment, but that's where my mind went. I quickly continued my run towards Wall Street and when I got there, I stopped to catch my breath. I couldn't run any further.

I could still hear the low rumbling low noise coming from behind me. I turned around and saw a huge wave of dark clouds and debris barreling toward where I was standing.

I continued my breathless run toward the eastern end of Wall Street and then ran inside one of the buildings on my left. Standing there, watching the wave of smoke, dust and debris passing by, I started to comprehend the magnitude of what had just happened. The horror I was witnessing was more than my mind could handle and slipped into shock trying as I tried to understand what was happening.

Next, my thoughts turned to my loved ones at home in NJ, my daughters and my wife, Maya. I knew Maya would see the news and realize that I was right in the heart of the storm. I imagined her frantic with worry but afraid to leave work. She was interning as a social worker.

For the first time in my life, I didn't feel secure and the consequences of terrorism seeped in. *It can't happen in America! We're a free nation!* I thought, but I still felt as violated as a mouse held in a trap, and definitely not free. I stayed there for about 20 minutes and then I walked down to my office, finding my way through the thick dust clouds by walking close to the buildings' outer walls. After reaching my building, I went directly up to speak with my boss, Tim.

"Tim! You have to let everyone go home or at least bring them down to the first floor!" I told him frantically. "I just saw Tower #1 of the Twin Towers collapse and I can still hear airplanes above." Tim was thought about for a while. In this era of "time is money" letting everyone leave for the day was a big decision. After about 15 minutes, he decided to relieve the employees on his team gradually.

After seeing that my coworkers were free to go home, I again went down to street level and walked up Wall Street. The air was dense with debris and smoke. I could hardly see more than a few feet ahead of me. Just before I got to Trinity Church, I saw a policewoman weeping and wringing her hands. I asked her what was happening and she said that there had been thousands of people inside when the tower collapsed.

I continued walking up and down the street, dazed, confused and shocked. I had never experienced an event of that magnitude, even when I was in the service. Then I heard the same rumbling and buckling metals sounding again, and I right away understood that the North Tower was collapsing as well.

I immediately turned and ran back to my building. This time, there were larger pieces of debris hurtling through the dense clouds of smoke and dust. After staying in my office for about 45 minutes, I decided to go outside once again.

Instead of leaving and going home like most sane people would have done, I decided to see if I could offer any help. I was trying to convince myself and find reasons to stay here in the center of the storm, but the reasons just didn't make sense. I was a financial center employee, not part of the rescue or military personnel, but I couldn't go home.

I walked up Wall Street surrounded by a thick fog of dust. My vision was limited to several feet maximum and at this point I hardly saw another person. I walked for some time. The few people who passed by me looked like ghosts because of all the dust covering them from head to toe. I assumed I looked that way too.

Every person I passed was silent, and none of us stopped to talk. The only sounds were police and fire sirens crying in anguish. I decided to turn back and go home. There wasn't a thing left for me to do. I took one of the last ferries home and just stood on its upper deck staring toward Manhattan.

I knew that the USA would never be the same after this horrendous attack. I started a conversation with a fellow passenger, saying, "This is like Pearl Harbor, but this time the casualties weren't military, they were hardworking civilians."

"The people who did it have awakened a giant sleeping bear and they will pay for it," he replied.

I didn't see Maya when I got home, and she didn't call me. I decided to wash off all dirt, dust and other muck that had rained down on me ask I walked. The tar had a peculiar smell, and reminded me of burning chicken feathers when my mother used to clean the chickens manually when I was a child. I threw all my clothes including my underwear into the trash and went for a long shower that lasted nearly an hour.

When Maya arrived later, I approached her and hugged her. I said that I saw the Twin Towers collapse. I was looking for some sympathy and care from her. I told her that thousands died in when the buildings collapsed. I was begging subconsciously for a hug or some support, but instead, Maya just coldly said, "*You're* alive aren't you?"

I felt deep contempt for Maya's response. For the first time in our relationship I felt that Maya really didn't care about me.

In 2002, a year after the September 11 terror attack, I lost my high-paying software consulting job. New York and New Jersey had become flooded with cheap H-1 visa workers who slowly replaced US citizens as information technology professionals — they were cheaper labor. I was out of work for nearly two years and we had to sell our expensive house and move to a smaller place in Marlboro, NJ. Maya chose the house and it seemed that she was happy there.

CHAPTER TWELVE

Maya's Affair

Maya finished her internship and got her first job as a psychologist, with the help of her internship supervisor, Dr. Rosensthal. She started work as a junior psychologist in a New Jersey jail and several days after she started her job there, she asked me not to call her when she was at work.

Maya started corresponding with her internship supervisor and went to meet him several times after she started this new job. One day, I came home early and found her laptop open and read her emails. It seemed that she had gone to lunch with her internship supervisor, and had done so several times in the past. I got angry that she didn't tell me she'd met him on one of her days off.

I was blinded by rage and couldn't think clearly. I accused Maya of lying and deception and I went as far as to suggest she was having an emotional affair with this Dr. Rosensthal. In response, Maya fixated on the fact that I'd read her emails and said it was a violation, comparing it to a rape. I'd never read her emails before and she had added a password to her account. I couldn't understand why she felt so violated, since she'd left the browser open to the email program — it wasn't like I'd broken into her account.

Later she told me her supervisor Dr. Rosensthal was understanding and he listened to her. "He's patient with me and compassionate," she said, implying that I wasn't. When I heard her remarks about Dr. Rosensthal, it felt like someone was stabbing me, and I an intense anger toward the man. I couldn't think logically and blamed my relationship problems on him.

When I calmed down, she told me she had filed for a divorce. I was devastated. I knew there were problems, and now I knew Maya had been working toward her independence. I just didn't expect it to happen so quickly.

Maya had always said that she wanted family and security, and here she was ready to break lose all that. She accused me of having several negative psychological traits and said that was why our marriage didn't work. She encouraged me to seek psychological help to correct these problems. I thought that Maya and I had communication and trust issues, but that was it. I couldn't understand her strong and immediate desire to get a divorce.

I wasn't convinced that she really didn't want to work on our marriage. I thought maybe her new job was stressful and perhaps this was causing her to behave differently.

In late December on a mild winter day, I drove to Maya's work in the afternoon. I intended to surprise her with a beautiful bouquet of long-stemmed roses. I drove to the jail where she worked as a psychologist and told the guard who I was and asked him to let Maya know her husband was waiting outside. The officer called Maya and let her know I was there, and then he dispatched a police officer with a car to lead me to her location.

When Maya came out, I waved to her. She seemed to be angry and ignored me. She went to her Jeep and drove off. I was deeply disappointed and I realized that she wasn't happy with my romantic gesture. I opened the window and threw the bunch of roses out.

This had finally opened my eyes to the real status of my marriage. Maya really wanted a divorce and she was making up excuses to make me feel that I was at fault.

I wasn't served with divorce papers, even though Maya said she had filed for a divorce. In retrospect, I should have noticed the changes in my wife as soon as she started working at that jail. The truth was, I just didn't want to see that my marriage was over. I always hurried back home to pick up my children, prepare their dinner and then help them with their homework, while Maya was usually worked late at work or had to go to her school to meet some other people.

It seemed like a fair exchange to me, but I was confused as to what role I had in this family since my wife completely ignored me. I took care of the children, but I also went to work to provide, while my spouse was getting ahead in her life without participating in the family.

Eventually she decided that her paychecks would go to her private account instead of the joint household account. By then, it was obvious changes were in the air.

One day directly after dinner I went out, and drove to a friend's house. He'd once worked in a marriage counseling office; I felt I could talk to him. I told telling him what was going on and that I felt something was wrong.

"She's having an affair," he said, "smell the coffee! You should get a private detective to give you a report so you'll finally know the truth. You can afford it!"

I was shattered by what he said, since it confirmed my worst doubts. It was quite clear to me what my friend meant.

I hired a private eye that proved my friend's theory. Maya would never suspect I, her gullible husband, could do such a thing. A week later, I got a report from the detective. While I was in Canada visiting my brother for the weekend, Maya and a man seemed to be together on a wintry Sunday night, in Millburn, a romantic New Jersey town. They spent four hours together at a restaurant/bar and then left, holding hands. That Sunday evening Maya had said she was scheduled for the evening shift at work.

I wanted to see Maya and talk with her, but I was just so angry. I climbed down the wooden steps leading to our first floor, and then stood on the first step overlooking the living room and kitchen. From there, I could see Maya seated on the loveseat with her legs propped on the small bench in front of her.

"Maya, I'd like to talk with you," I said in a low-toned, quivering whisper.

"Not, now. Don't you see I'm busy?"

"Maya, I know you're having an affair," I said, quickly returning to my usual tone of voice. "Don't bother denying it; I had a detective follow you."

Maya jumped off the loveseat like snake bit her behind, and went into her typical rage. She yelled for several minutes, startling our children, and then she called my brother and accused him of financing the detective. She couldn't believe that hiring a detective had been my idea.

The next day I was notified by a police officer that Maya was trying to get a temporary restraining order against me and he advised me to find another place to live. He could see the writing on the proverbial wall. The divorce complaint was served to me the next day, and I realized I really did have to leave the house. The temporary restraining order was served one day later.

My first days in my new, empty apartment were lonely. I had to buy furniture; I'd slept on the floor for the first few days. I went several times to my house along with police escort to get some of my personal belongings; however, except for clothing, I wasn't allowed to remove anything else.

Mr. Rosen was hired as my attorney for the divorce process; I picked him using the yellow pages. He was an older gentleman who was beyond middle age. He was stiff, with a sour and sarcastic sense of humor. His office was on the commercial side of Route 33. His location gave a clue as to how much he wanted to spend on office rent. His office was located about five miles away from the Monmouth courthouse, and looked like a renovated manufacturing plant.

I entered the building and went directly to his office, skipping conversation with his paralegal and secretary. He began talking to me as soon as I got to his doorway, telling me about the services he could offer. I stood there short of his entering and scanned his office.

He sat there behind a big old desk that seemed to be older than he was. In front of the desk was a wooden chair, obviously from another set of office furniture, used as seating for his clients. I glanced at his face and didn't exactly feel he was trustworthy. With some amusement he returned my stare and we smiled.

I entered his office and sat on the old wooden chair. Mr. Rosen looked like a man in his late 60s and was gave the impression of being extremely busy. There was a slight pause after I explained why I was there, then he asked, "Are you *sure* you want to file for a divorce?"

He scrutinized me as I answered, "Yes, I'm sure, because my wife is sure. I was already served with the divorce papers."

Mr. Rosen just nodded his head and said, "In divorce there are no winners. It's the children of divorce who lose the most."

Mr. Rosen set up an agreement for me to see my children regularly. I was supposed to pay temporary child support and alimony during this time as well. I found it strange that I was ordered to pay alimony to a woman who was making more than I did.

I hoped to get scheduled visitations with my children and the Judge assigned to our divorce did order biweekly visitations. However, Maya's vindictive nature made her want to control my visitations at any cost. On several occasions when I was talking with my daughters on the phone, Maya took the phone from them and yelled profanities at me. She also threatened that if I didn't pay all the house bills she would completely stop my visits with the children.

CHAPTER THIRTEEN

Dr. Psylie, Court Appointed Custody Evaluator

I told Judge Irish that I wanted physical custody of my children. I thought I should try to get custody because of Maya's behavior, visitations disturbances and the fact that she hardly spent time with our children. In retrospect it was one of the greatest mistakes I made in my life, and perhaps the very greatest mistake any man could make while going through a divorce in the current legal system.

The court rarely awards custody to men, even though the laws in New Jersey are written with apparent equal rights regarding this issue. Furthermore, a man requesting custody invites himself to a losing battle that will make many lawyers richer through legal and consulting fees. Mostly all these highly paid court-appointed consultants all will arrive at the same conclusion — the mother will always have physical custody. This was the case with Dr. Psylie, the court appointed custody evaluator. I vividly remember my first meeting with Dr. Psylie.

I woke up early that morning in anticipation of my first meeting with Dr. Psylie, the court-appointed custody evaluator. I hadn't slept well, worry about this meeting and the memories of the previous day's audit with the IRS had contributed to my restless night. I was irritable and worried, but knew I needed to get ready for the meeting. I looked around my room and felt disgust. "It's just not my home," I said to myself.

Dr. Psylie's office was located in a house. I was surprised, since I'd got the impression her practice was located in one of the office buildings in Freehold, when I spoke to her on the phone. This is the same Freehold that Bruce Springsteen sang about. It used to be a white, working-class town but slowly turned into something else, with many houses downtown converted to offices that served as extensions of the Monmouth County courthouse.

Dr. Psylie seemed to be practicing out of her home, with two of its rooms converted to consultation and reception space. I entered the reception room at the side of the house. It had an old white early last century working-class appearance with some paintings hanging on the walls — they all had streaming water as their main motif. The room had a bit of Western European flavor represented by shabby old European-style furniture and the flowery yellow wallpaper.

In the center of the room were two old wooden chairs sorely in need of varnishing, and a square wooden table that had some children's storybooks and old periodicals lying on top. An ancient orange sofa occupied most of the western side of the room. It was draped with a flowery cover that tried to hide how faded the upholstery was.

Dr. Psylie opened her office door and greeted me. "David?" she asked with a serious, stern look.

"Yes, I'm David Tal. It's nice to meet you."

Dr. Psylie stared at me and seemed to be forming opinions about me already, so I just gazed blankly at her, trying to demonstrate my self-confidence. I followed her to her office and sat down on the small couch that seemed the younger brother of the orange monstrosity in the reception area.

Her office was decorated in a similar manner to the reception area, and I could hear the heavy breathing of a large dog behind the side door. That seemed to confirm that she did in fact live here as well.

I sat down and continued my blank gaze at her, making no sound, as though I was there just to listen. Dr. Psylie was an anemic-looking woman in her late fifties with blond hair arranged in a strange Medusa-like style. She was dressed conservatively in a long out-of-fashion blue skirt. She continued her staring match, watching me intently with her cold, piercing blue eyes.

I got the impression she'd never had children and was getting a significant lesbian vibe from her. It felt strange to be evaluated for custody by someone who probably didn't have kids, but she was one of the most respectable psychologists in the arsenal of the Monmouth court so I didn't have much choice.

Dr. Psylie started describing her services to me in a monotone, robot-like voice. She didn't pause between sentences, so there was no time for a response from me.

"Did you receive the information I sent?" I finally asked when she took a breath.

Instead of replying, Dr. Psylie leaned forward, put her hands on the table and then gazed momentarily at the ceiling. This response completely confused me, so I tried to stare inquisitively at her, as if expecting her to speak at some point. I realized that Maya had already had her session with Dr. Psylie and had apparently swayed the good doctor in her favor.

Dr. Psylie decided to give me an answer, "Yes I received the information and I read it."

I shrugged my shoulders when I heard the tone of her reply.

"Do you know that airline pilots score high in narcissistic traits?" she asked rather sarcastically.

"I'm not an airline pilot, I was an Air Force officer many years ago," I said falteringly. "I don't understand the connection you're trying to make."

Dr. Psylie moved her blank stare away from me, crossed her legs to the left of the table and lowered her head. She didn't answer, because she knew she had crossed a line in her analysis as a custody evaluator. "No need to be annoyed," Dr. Psylie blurted out. "These are just general statistics and in no way have any effect on this evaluation. I do different analyses, interviews and I see your children. My opinions are based only on this data."

"Thank you. But I still think that my Air Force past has nothing to do with this evaluation." I paused for a moment, my mind was racing. I stared into Dr. Psylie's cold blue eyes and without stopping to catch a breath told her, "I decided to request a custody evaluation knowing the cost involved and realizing that my chances, based on statistics, are low because I'm a man.

"I made this request because I'm not sure that it's in the best interest of my children to be with their mother. I stated those reasons. I don't want to cause the children any more stress than necessary. I think we can do this by keeping things as close to what they're used to as possible.

"They were with me most of the time and only spent one or two evenings a week they spent with the mother. Different people are taking care of them now, and my ex-spouse has the same schedule. Why does she need custody if she's not willing to spend more time with them?"

Dr. Psylie sat there wearing a stern look. She then looked at the ground as she spoke, "You have to understand that I'm not taking sides, I'm doing what's best for the children."

Dr. Psylie then proceeded with her formal approach and asked me to describe my relationship with my spouse. This gave me free reign to air my grievances. I enjoyed the whining session, and I was a bit relieved to know that someone was listening who could have the power to change this out-of-control chain of events.

I basically retold all that I had written in the manuscript in a concise way, stopping and emphasizing all the dramatic events in our past. Dr. Psylie rarely interrupted me and I enjoyed the freedom she gave me to describe the things that happened to me.

Suddenly I realized she was writing notes as I talked. I'd been so absorbed in my laments that I hadn't noticed until now. I figured she was writing down my responses to specific events and interpreting my body language as I described those events.

When she realized I'd stopped talking, she announced a 10-minute break. I went out to her waiting room while she went inside to attend to her "family." I'd heard her dog getting more and more restless on the other side of the door. It must've been time to take him for a walk.

After the short break, Dr. Psylie invited me back into her office. Her eyes were shining with cold brilliance and she had an uneasy smile on her lips. "Do you really think that the fact that your wife is a Psychologist will weigh in this evaluation?" she asked quietly.

"Probably. I'm not familiar with this process and I don't have a team of psychologists to coach me on this process like she does," I answered.

Dr. Psylie didn't respond to this statement.

I wanted to carry on the theme of domestic violence that had been suggested in the motions my wife submitted to the court using the manuscript I'd written as a basis. I wanted to demonstrate to Dr. Psylie that domestic violence can happen to men as well, and that what my wife was doing was a farce.

I knew it would be a hard sell, as Dr. Psylie seemed to be a middle-aged remnant of the feminist seventies. However, I tried to make her understand anyway. "I know that psychological and physical violence has an effect on both men and women, and I want you to know that I was treated as an abused spouse by the Marlboro Crisis Intervention Service. There was a history of violence committed by my spouse, and to my credit I never reciprocated." I paused there and then sank back into the sofa.

"What do you mean, domestic violence committed by your wife?" she asked with disbelief.

"You'll understand very well when you hear some of the recording."

"I'll understand? We'll see," Dr. Psylie said skeptically. She paused then and gave me some time to respond.

I thought maybe Dr. Psylie was starting to show some emotion; her body language was extremely tense. She was losing her poker face as she bent forward to listen.

"She was in the habit of shouting loudly and endlessly without apparent reason. Our neighbors can testify to that fact. She called me names in Russian and in English, and she used insulting adjectives such as idiot, stupid, etc. and she did this in front of our children. On the physical side she'd started kicking, scratching and punching me lately."

"No! ...No," Dr. Psylie whispered to herself in a tone that sounded naive and disbelieving. Looking up she seemed to realize she'd said that out loud, then told me to continue.

I paused for some time as though I needed time to recover and gather my thoughts. "She psychologically abused me, targeting my feelings, emotions and self-esteem. She called me fat, even though I'm not. She told everyone that I don't have money or a pension and I'm worthless. She also told my brother that I'm too old and she doesn't have anything in common with me, nothing to talk about."

"Can this really be true?" Dr. Psylie whispered again in disbelief.

"Yes, it's true. She also wanted me to make more money, suggesting I'm not making enough, when she was the one spending all my money. She knew just how much to spend not to get into heavy debt, but still make sure she depleted my savings. She also abused my oldest daughter, attacking her verbally and physically. I felt totally powerless to interfere because when I tried she would start yelling and physically attacking me."

Dr. Psylie stared at me with anguish. "What you're telling me is the truth?"

"Yes," I answered. "Men don't usually admit to being physically abused by a woman. However, I wanted you to know what type of a person my spouse is so that you don't give her custody of our children."

"You'd better tell me everything that's happened in the last several months...without examples," she said.

I turned to her, looked deep into her eyes and put my hands on the table. "You don't know what it feels like to know that your wife is out with someone else. You can't comprehend what I felt when she was disappearing from the house without explanation or saying she was working late at the jail and not getting home until after midnight. She told me she didn't have to explain anything to me. She also locked me out of her bedroom."

I paused for a second, staring at Dr. Psylie, looking for some signs that I was getting through to her, but there was nothing. "She also refused to communicate with me unless she wanted me to pay the bills or correct her work."

Dr. Psylie shrugged and almost inaudibly uttered, "Let's leave the rest for the next session."

I cordially thanked Dr. Psylie and left. I had a bad feeling about this session and about this psychologist and I wished I could someone else to do it. I couldn't realistically expect a Dr. Psylie to write a negative evaluation about one of her fellow psychologists.

Later that afternoon I faxed the following letter to Dr. Psylie:

> Dr. Psylie,
> *If you think that at this stage I shouldn't worry about my ex-spouse's behavior or that I do not have a chance of getting physical custody, please let me know and I'll request suspension of this evaluation. If you think at this stage that something is wrong with my behavior, please let me know what I should do about it. I will do what you recommend in order to correct it, as I do not have physical custody anyway.*
>
> *I have verbally demonstrated my intense discontent at my ex-spouse's conduct. I know it may not be relevant to the evaluation. However, I would like you to understand that I couldn't comprehend that my dedication, loyalty and support of my ex-spouse and my children would turn into the biggest possible betrayal and humiliation. It happened suddenly and explosively, and sadly in our children's presence.*
>
> *Our children's involvement in this process is the most disturbing fact. I know that you're measuring my responses. I want this evaluation to be fair and correct and I'll not hide behind any mask.*
>
> *Yes, I'm upset; my visitation had been revoked. I'm being accused of having a mental illness and of committing domestic violence. My children have been turned against*

me. I was always even-tempered and even-mannered — ask anyone who knows me.

In addition, the video my daughter took that I played for you shows my ex-spouse going into a shouting rampage and that I was just trying to contain myself. I'm afraid for my children and worry what's happening to them, but my hands are tied. I didn't hesitate to verbally state my frustrations at your session, and I hope you will interpret these reactions correctly.

Respectfully
David Tal

CHAPTER FOURTEEN

Dr. Psylie — Second Appointment

I woke up a bit later than usual this morning, following a restless night's sleep often interrupted by my uneasy anticipation of the second meeting with Dr. Psylie. I hurriedly dressed and then ran towards my car. I realized I couldn't pin my hopes on this doctor I hardly knew.

I couldn't understand my fascination with Dr. Psylie, it was like I thought she had some hidden power over my life, which she ultimately did. I was wound up and tense while driving to my appointment. I knew my main worry was that my ex-wife was manipulating the good doctor. There was certainly nothing I could see with Dr. Psylie that told me she hadn't succeeded.

I just had to hope that Dr. Psylie was a professional who could see through the lies. The whole process still worried me. If they did have a professional alliance then it would affect the accuracy of this evaluation and ruin any chance I had at a happy future with my children. I'd already been denied visitation for the last six months, and I couldn't take much more.

I approached Dr. Psylie's waiting room door and knocked timidly. She opened it and greeted me.

"I'm glad to see you again," I said warmly.

"I know, I know!" Dr. Psylie responded suddenly with ironic vexation.

The doubt about Dr. Psylie's neutrality came back immediately at her response, but I said nothing and followed her to her office.

Meanwhile Dr. Psylie turned a little toward me and began staring at me with curiosity, as though she had never seen me before. There was something peculiar in her appearance, something that seemed to contradict her title.

"I hope you're not nervous," she said loudly.

"No, I'm fine. I haven't seen my children for a long time, so I want this to go well. I miss them and worry that they're in harm's way. My spouse's mother, who is anti-Semitic and difficult, is caring for them. I feel helpless and I can't do anything about it. My hands are tied."

"What do you mean your hands are tied?" Dr. Psylie asked with marked curiosity.

"I heard that my youngest daughter, Anika, was nearly run over by a car. My oldest daughter mocked my religion and made fun of Passover during a phone conversation with me."

Dr. Psylie moved backwards suddenly; her legs jerked to the left and were completely hidden under the desk. She licked her lips nervously several times, and at that moment I knew she was also Jewish. She had felt what anti-Semitism means, and was uncomfortable to hearing about it. Suddenly we had something in common — anti-Semitism.

"I know you don't like tape recordings," I told Dr. Psylie. "However, one of my lawyers, Mr. Sucker, told me to tape everything because my spouse has been recording things since the beginning."

Dr. Psylie didn't respond.

"This recording follows my daughter's brain-washing about Jews. She's mocking Jewish celebrations and making fun of my religion. She never did that while I was at home, since most of her family members are Jewish."

I opened my recorder and played the conversation I'd had with my daughter.

David: *"Who told you that? Who told you that? That you want to do what?"*

Ally: "I don't like celebrating Passover (mockingly sings) Hava nagila hava... Hava nagila hava... and do all kinds of disgusting things."

"This commend is because my spouse and her mother believed that Jews drink blood at Passover!" I added sarcastically and with a grim smile.

"Do you want me to play some more?" I asked slowly, as though I was serving her an item from a menu.

"Yes," she answered faintly.

"I'll play you the tape of the Dec. 29 incident, when my spouse managed to evict me claiming I hit her. You can decide for yourself what really happened. She was yelling at me about money in front of my daughters, then she shoved me out the door. This is an ultimate low for me, after providing for my family for 11 years and spending hundreds of thousands on my spouse's education, and her high standard of living. Once she started working, her new source of income went into her private bank account."

Dr. Psylie just sat there silently and continuously wrote on her notepad. I wasn't sure what she was writing, but I hoped she had some sympathy for my plight. I really wanted this grave-faced woman to understand who my spouse really is.

I started the second tape and Dr. Psylie just sat there listening quietly and taking notes. *She definitely has a poker face*, I thought.

After playing the tape up to the point where the police arrived, I stopped it and looked at Dr. Psylie. "The police arrived and the rest of what had happened is described in my manuscript."

Dr. Psylie jumped from her loveseat and crossed to the other side of her office. In the corner there was a small bookshelf and she pulled out the thickest book from that shelf. She opened the book and started reading quietly.

I felt inclined to start a conversation with her as to the contents of that book. However, she didn't take any notice of me, and continued reading quietly as though I didn't exist. She then turned around and stared at my face in deep thought, and headed back to her loveseat.

I felt strangely attracted to this woman, not to her physical looks but to her intellect and authoritative manner. Somehow I found myself thinking how it would be dancing with her to blaring music in a fancy club, following her steps in high-heeled shoes that I couldn't think she was capable of wearing. I brushed off these strange thoughts as patient–therapist dependency.

"David? Let's continue."

I jolted back to reality and what the objective of this session was. "You know the most sensational feelings I've had in the last several months were real pain and a sense of loss and betrayal. I felt physical pain and physical discomfort; I thought Maya's mother was poisoning me. I continuously felt tightness in my stomach and constant muscular pain. The pain was real but doctors couldn't find anything wrong other than possibly acid reflux. I felt perpetual fear and was constantly 'on guard' from her dangerous mother. I didn't have control of anything, I felt inadequate and I often accepted my spouse's constant denigrations. I lost my self-esteem and my self-confidence. These things were noticed by my extended family and it worried them a great deal."

Dr. Psylie just sat there scribbling away, without showing any emotions or different body language. She knew I was tracking her responses, and she tried her best to hide any visible clues to her reactions.

I handed Dr. Psylie a note I'd been holding in my hand for the last twenty minutes and said, "I was trying to reconcile with her and complete this divorce amicably. I was doing that in the interest of our children. In response, she submitted that peaceful note to the police saying it was harassment. I don't know if she has any capability to feel and that scares me as she's now the sole caretaker of my children."

The note read:

"I was with you for 11 years and we have two children together. I did care for you unconditionally and I'm hurt by what has happened. I don't want to fight with you in any way through the legal system. When our children grow up they will remember all of this, and I want to minimize their exposure. What we're doing now isn't providing good parenting.

I know you want a divorce, and I'll cooperate with you. I want to come to a compromise with you using least legal intervention possible. Most lawyers will be interested in keeping us in conflict, with tensions high, because they make more money that way.

Tomorrow is our first time in court and I know you have a lawyer; so do I. I don't want to face you in court. I always treated you right and stood by you. You and your mother are directing anger at the wrong person (look to your father, who deserted you when you were a child, if you want to place blame).

Please take a moment to think and remember we still are the parents of the same children."

Dr. Psylie read the note quickly and then put it aside, as though it didn't have any relevance. Then she said, "Our time is up. We'll continue this next time."

Later on that evening I wrote another letter to Dr. Psylie

Dear Dr. Psylie,

I spent seven years as an Air Force officer and was married to Maya for 10 years. I have never responded to any domestic problems with violence; on the contrary, I responded with understanding and support.

I said this before, and I repeat it again. I requested this evaluation because I'm not sure my spouse is capable of maintaining physical custody and giving the emotional support that our children need. I'm also sure that if she has full physical custody, I'll never see my children again. She has not cooperated with me during any part of this divorce proceeding, nor did she follow court orders. On the other hand, I would never stop the mother of my children from seeing them.

I'm willing to go to any parenting classes suggested. I'm also willing to take any therapy suggested to reduce the bad feeling and intense discontent I have regarding my ex-spouse's conduct on how my marriage ended.

As I mentioned, Maya's schedule is beyond hectic. She leaves the house at 6:45 a.m. and comes home at 12:45 a.m. on a daily basis, 5 days a week. The sixth day was her only normal workday, when she would get home at 6 p.m. The valuable free time she has is spent on school work, and on Saturdays, the only day she could spend quality time at home, she's usually at the mall shopping to a tune of $4K a month, or busy doing homework.

Her schedule is still the same. I worry that she has little time to spend with our children.

Respectfully
David Tal

CHAPTER FIFTEEN

Mr. Muller — Court Appointed Reunification Therapist

After six months, the period that I was prevented from seeing my children except when I briefly met them through Dr. Psylie, the presiding family Judge, Judge Irish ordered a meeting with the children through a Reunification Therapist suggested by my spouse's lawyer. I accepted this, as there was no other alternative presented to me in order to see my children again.

On one Thursday evening I went to meet my daughters' Reunification Therapist, Mr. Muller, and I was happy I could meet him. I knew that the meeting was just a personal face-to-face meeting but I knew it would finally lead me to meet my daughters. This is what the Judge wanted and I agreed with this arrangement, as I knew otherwise my daughters would be completely alienated and would not want to see me.

Mr. Muller was a good-looking man in his late 40s who seemed to smile a lot. He didn't seem to be a very smart man and was slow in his talk, although he seemed blissfully and completely happy to be in this profession. Mr. Muller was a little out of breath, and his red tie was inappropriately pulled behind his back. He seemed slightly nervous to meet me, and I felt certain that I was going to disagree with him and the process he wanted to apply in order for me to reinstate visitations.

He had a rather astonishing set of green eyes, and a full head of dark brown hair covering his entire scalp, which may have added to his appearance as a middle-aged attractive man. Somehow his appearance was in a sense indicative of his personality and attitude towards the opposite sex. He was well-dressed in a custom-tailored suit, something I wouldn't expect a child therapist could afford.

I spent one hour with Mr. Muller, half of which was devoted to me complaining about my inability to get visitation with my children. I repeated the same information I'd presented to Dr. Psylie. When I was done complaining, he assured me that he'd heard similar complaints from every other man who needed his services. It seemed to me that any professional in this business has the same non-reaction to these issues and reserved the apparent compassion and understating for the one who is paying them.

While conversing with Mr. Muller, he showed me a book he was reading — something spiritual about God and the meaning of life. I took this as meaning I was supposed to think there was something more to this guy because of what he was reading.

Who knows? Maybe he really did have good intentions and wasn't an agent working for my ex-spouse's attorney, even though he was requested by her and his services were court-ordered by Judge Irish.

I looked at him and said, "You know I've written something that may be of interest to you. It's about creation and evolution and it includes physical, psychological, medical and philosophical reasons to explain why creation is a fact." I handed him a copy of the essay I'd written several years ago. I always carry several copies in my briefcase.

He looked at me and said, "Yes, I do believe that we all have one God and there is no difference between denominations."

I answered, "Yes we all have one God, but after my experiences with this divorce I also believe that there is a devil at work."

He seemed startled by this revelation, and looked at me for several seconds before asking, "What do you mean?"

"Exactly what you heard," I replied. "My ex-spouse's behavior is the manifestation of evil; there's no other way I can explain her actions. No mother would willingly put her children through this process and isolate them from their father knowing the psychological damage it's causing. She's a trained psychologist, after all."

Mr. Muller paused for several seconds and then changed the subject.

Yes, we were here to talk about my daughter and what I should do not to keep from alienating her. It seems that every professional in the divorce business assumes that the man is the cause of everything wrong in the relationship, and is the cause of the divorce and alienating his children.

"Mr. Muller, you have to understand, I didn't get visitation with my children. The alienation started *after* I left home. Please, tell me how I could have possibly caused it."

He just stared at me for a while and didn't answer. After a minute or two he exclaimed in a conciliatory voice, "You have to stop talking negatively about your spouse when you're around your children!"

"I may have occasionally responded to my daughters' unfounded accusations about me on the phone, but I assume that's a normal reaction when one is accused of something he didn't do."

"You have to understand that your oldest daughter doesn't want to see you. She's angry with you," Mr. Muller responded aggressively.

"If my spouse hadn't made insurmountable obstacles to my visitation and didn't use our children to get back at me for whatever reasons she has, I would be calmer and more careful when I talk around my children."

It was then that Mr. Muller dropped his bombshell. "I've recommended to the Judge that you shouldn't see your children for several months."

I was angry and deeply disappointed. Apparently he was an "agent" working for my spouse after all. "Why did you do that? You did it without even meeting me!" I said in a shocked voice.

"I did it because your daughter seemed to be extremely angry with you and didn't want to see you," he explained weakly.

"Do you have any clue what parental alienation is?" I asked.

"I'm have some knowledge on this issue and I'm waiting for Dr. Psylie's recommendation on what to do," Mr. Muller answered with noticeable unease, as he had just stated his professional lacking.

I got up and thanked Mr. Muller for the session. He asked me to pay for the session and insisted on being paid immediately after each session, suggesting that I should request reimbursement from my insurance. I felt uneasy while writing the check, but I knew I had no choice if I wanted to ever see my children again. I later learned that Muller was a defrocked Catholic priest who left the church to marry.

Later that evening I drove through Highway 35 and passed by the "Go-Go Club." It's a fancy dump where girls show their naked bodies for tips. I paid the cover charge to a guy with a greasy face who was acting as gatekeeper. The music was loud and the place was dimly lit. I saw several scantily clad girls with their high-tech tits on display. Their plastic boobies were juicy, firm and large, much larger than my spouse's.

Everywhere I looked, there were more surgically enhanced breasts bouncing around. I finally took a seat next to the runway that looked sort of like those you'd see at a fashion show. This was no fashion show, though!

There were several girls, some of whom liked the models I'd seen on magazine covers, but these "models" weren't wearing clothes. They were all really strutting their naked stuff!

The music switched to "One Night in Bangkok" a released in 1984 by Murray Head. Yes! It felt just like I was in Bangkok, not in some town in suburban New Jersey.

A tall blond girl started dancing on the runway. She stopped in front of me and then her boobs were an inch away from my face. Up close, they looked really fake as they were waved in circles in front of my face. The woman stepped back and opened her legs wide. I could see everything, and I was surprised at the gesture. Seeing a strange woman's genitals this close-up did *not* turn me on.

I was perversely hypnotized by the site, though, and pointed my finger toward her center and asked, "What's that?"

The girl was startled by this question and she asked "What did you say, honey?"

I again said, "What's that, ma'am?" pointing my finger again at the center of her exposed genitalia.

"This is the center of the earth," she said, and then she gasped and continued, "This is where you want to park your car and then go play merry-go-around."

I was surprised by her answer and I gave her a $5 note. "Thank you," she said and continued dancing.

I suddenly saw my spouse dancing. I knew it couldn't be, but it seemed she was popping behind the dancers. She seemed to have red eyes and horns. I was trying to focus my eyes and I rubbed them against my fist. "It can't be," I said to myself. Suddenly a tall brunette started dancing next to me. She was completely naked except for her shoes, the heels of which were narrow and tall as any I'd ever seen.

She started swinging her massive breasts and I raised my finger and asked her, "Got milk?"

The dancer didn't understand and didn't answer. "What's your name?" I asked.

"Shantel," she replied in a husky voice.

"Shantel, or show and tell?" I replied.

Shantel looked nervous and annoyed, so I shoved $5 between her tits. "Thank you" she replied and continued dancing.

I suddenly saw my spouse staring at me with those red burning eyes and her horns were moving from side to side. I got up and started walking toward the exit. Shantel followed me and asked, "Do you want a private dance with me, honey?" She was going after me completely naked and I just stared at her.

"No, I do not," I replied and quickly exited the Go-Go Club. I could feel Shantel's scorn hitting my back as I ran to my car. I started it quickly headed through the exit. I quietly said, "Thank God I'm out of that place!" It didn't make sense to say that, but it did make me feel better.

I realized that a woman I don't have feelings for, who doesn't have feelings for me, means nothing to me. Not physically, not emotionally and not financially.

CHAPTER SIXTEEN

Early Military Life

The Court Officer suddenly moved to the other side of the courtroom, went down on his knees in front of the Judge's door and picked up some document from the floor. I realized I was still in the courtroom waiting for the Judge to return and render her Judgment. My thoughts took me back to a period over 20 years ago when I was seated in a similar room at my air force base. I was in the briefing room just before our day's mission. The memories started flowing…

It was a beautiful day and I knew something was going to happen. I was called in on emergency and the briefing was hurried. I took off with my wing leader and I was now flying up high in the Northern direction. I was only in radio contact with our wing leader and the controller. The controller was some unknown young girl who had a pleasant, calming voice; we relied on the controllers because they alerted us on friends or enemies and gave us clues as to what to do. Her voice was soothing and I started imagining her. She was probably a tall brunette who came from an established family and was chosen for this duty because of her intelligence. She was pretty, I was assuming, based on the clearness and sweetness of her voice. Suddenly I heard her voice with an elevated tone, and I got startled.

"Enemy planes taking off 45 miles out in three groups of eight."

Then she repeated, sounding a bit hysterical but still relatively calm. *"I repeat, I repeat — enemy is taking off 45 miles away in three groups of eight."*

I then understood that the day was to be a day of action and real action was on schedule. I didn't know why so many enemy airplanes were up, but we knew that our commanders knew what they were doing and we explicitly trusted their actions and decisions. I switched on my ADF and put on one of the music channels, as I often listened to music while flying and this wasn't in our regulations. I looked around and saw the groups of enemy fighters approaching from the East. My wing commander knew what to do first. He just led us directly to them expecting them to break off, and then we would start the dog's dance. All the planes then would begin to circle each other with a series of high-speed turns, rolls and other aerobatic maneuvers. I just flew to the left of my wing commander and I saw my wing commander waving. I waved back and saluted. The first leading MIG was about 5 miles away and my wing commander took it head on. We followed him and each one of us knew which target we needed to take on, because our training specified the exact priorities of each of us. My ADF was playing one of the frequently broadcasted rock music songs, "Another One Bites the Dust" from the English rock band Queen. I started singing along:

> *"David walks warily down the street,*
> *With the brim pulled way down low*
> *Ain't no sound but the sound of his feet,*
> *Machine guns ready to go"*

I looked below and saw my first target. I performed a wing over followed by an inverse half a loop and then I was behind the MIG. I was above him and I had energy that he didn't, which enabled me to easily maneuver my machine behind him. I approached him, cutting the distance between us, and he still didn't notice me. I then squeezed the trigger, and I heard a faint "tang" and the missile was on its way. I continued singing with the same rhythm.

> *"Are you ready, are you ready for this?*
> *Are you hanging on the edge of your seat?"*

The missile hit the MIG and I continued humming...
"Out of the doorway the bullets rip
To the sound of the beat."

I saw the pilot eject and I sighed a sigh of relief. I then took a glimpse of my second target about two miles away and one of the other squadron's planes was pursuing him. I turned a steep turn to the right and positioned myself behind the MIG and ahead of the other guy. The other pursuing plane understood the gesture and then turned left and away.

"Another one bites the dust
Another one bites the dust
And another one gone, and another one gone
Another one bites the dust."

I was now about a mile behind the MIG and I was ready to send the second missile away.

"Hey, I'm gonna get you too
Another one bites the dust."

I selected the missile and squeezed the trigger.

"How do you think I'm going to get along,
Without you, when you're gone?
You took me for everything that I had,
And kicked me out on my own."

The MIG exploded into a red, blue, silver and black ball of fire and debris. I performed a steep climbing turn to the right to avoid hitting the debris. I looked out from the clear glass cockpit and saw that the sky was full of jets maneuvering and I could see one spiraling to the ground. Thank God it was a MIG, I was thinking to myself. I could easily identify who was a friend and who was the foe, and the identification was easy as it was imbedded into our brains with the silhouettes of the different types of enemy planes. The radio was noisy and I could hear warnings coming from all over. "No 2 behind you at 7 o'clock. No 4, 9 O'clock!" The only voice I listened to was the controller's voice. She was assigned to only four of us and at those moments no other voice mattered. I was still humming:

"Are you happy, are you satisfied?
How long can you stand the heat?"

We were better trained and we had better equipment. The Russian-produced top of the line MIG-25 wasn't a "performer" and many of them were shot down that day. With some altitude and extra potential energy I could easily out-maneuver this airplane... I was thinking. I saw another one about 5 miles away and 7,000 feet below me. The pilot was flying alone contemplating going back to his base. He was flying in an eastwardly direction and I was flying in the northwardly direction. With one barrel roll followed by a steep turning dive I was behind him and gaining speed. I continued singing while hearing the non-stop cries and commands on the radio.

"Out of the doorway the bullets rip
To the sound of the beat
Another one bites the dust
Another one bites the dust
Another one bites the dust
Another one bites the dust."

I was behind the enemy only 500 yards away in a shooting position and I squeezed the machine-gun's trigger. I squeezed for several seconds.

"Out of the doorway the bullets rip
Repeating the sound of the beat
Another one bites the dust
Another one bites the dust."

I saw pieces of metal ripping off the MIG and black smoke coming out from its tail. The Jet suddenly swerved to its right and entered into an uncontrolled spin. I continued humming,

> "There are plenty of ways you can hurt a man
> And bring him to the ground"
> "You can beat him
> You can cheat him
> You can treat him bad and leave him
> When he is down
> But I'm ready, yes I'm ready for you
> I'm standing on my own two feet."

I was singing loudly and I suddenly felt something pulling my hand. I looked to my left, saw it was my lawyer, and realized I was in Judge's Killmen's room waiting for her verdict.

CHAPTER SEVENTEEN

Guilty

JUDGE KILLMEN'S SUMMARY: "All right, in this case, I find that I, Judge Killmen, have jurisdiction to consider the matter. The parties are currently going through a very contentious divorce. The main issue seems to be child custody and parenting time, and this plaintiff has appeared at my (Judge Killmen's) court a number of times. I'm looking at what would be the second domestic violence file. Maya came to this court and sought a restraining order against David, filed on January 29th, this year in the Marlboro municipal court. And there she alleged that David handed her a copy of a manuscript and that the manuscript is essentially a description of their relationship. This caused her to be concerned.

As Judge Killmen read her summary, I counted off all the mistakes she had made in her assessment and judgment. But by the looks of this woman, and the way she coddled Maya and her family in questioning, I already felt as if I knew the results. The judge didn't mention that it was illegal to take a document from another therapist and present it publicly; neither had she thought that the action may point to a lack of morality or done in order to publicly humiliate me. The Judge continued her summary.

"So she filed for a temporary restraining order. That order was dismissed on February the 22nd this year. And on that very same date, a consent order for civil restraints was filed. That's marked P—1. And paragraph one of that Order filed under docket number FM44—444—99C says: number one: "It's hereby agreed that neither party shall have any communication with the other. The only communication that would be acceptable would be communication to deal with issues regarding the children. And those communications shall be done by e-mail between the parties only. There should be no verbal communication or other written communication between the parties."

"Number two, neither party shall have communication with any coworkers, friends or family of the other party.

"Number three, neither party shall stalk, follow or otherwise interfere with the daily activities of the other party. Each party is specifically prohibited from going to the other party's place of employment. Under this order, the plaintiff was granted exclusive use and possession of the marital residence.

"The parties agreed that they would have joint legal custody of the children. The defendant was to have parenting time with the children on Tuesdays and Sundays. And again, that was agreed to and the parties agreed that either of them could return to court with regard to any other issues. And so the plaintiff dismissed her temporary restraining order based upon this agreement that they would abide by the civil restraints.""

The judge was assuming in preparation for her verdict and that was wrong and not true. The opposing counsel requested dismissal as the counsel realized my spouse had no case, and my lawyer advised me to go forward with the civil restraint order! The Judge continued reading her verdict and I already assumed what the verdict would be. I couldn't believe I was seated in a court in the major democracy of the free world.

"Now, the plaintiff after filing that restraining order came to this court at the end of January and wrote in her request for a temporary restraining order that the defendant had followed her on January 15th and had been waiting outside her work. Then the plaintiff testified that since that time in January when the parties separated, the defendant had called her work at least once a week."

There was no proof submitted! All hearsay not allowable in court and still taken in.

"The defendant called her dentist. The defendant said the reason for that was he wanted to confirm that she was late for a reason to a particular appointment. The plaintiff testified that the defendant follows her. The last time was in October of this year after she left a mediation meeting. The defendant followed her on the Parkway and she could see his car behind her.

"She testified that on July the 14th, there was a situation where she was driving on Route 9 after she had dropped the children off from sessions with Dr. Psylie. She dropped the children off at home and then was on her way to work and the defendant cut her off and went around her car. According to her testimony, this almost caused an accident. She dialed #77 to report an aggressive driver. They told her to go back to the Marlboro police and tell them there was a problem."

I provided evidence that I was with Dr. Psylie at that time, which the Judge again ignored!

"The defendant seems to suggest through argument with, or argument espoused by, Todd Prone that the reason the plaintiff has brought this particular temporary restraining order request is because of a motion that's pending."

This and immigration issues which she didn't allow!

"And yet, Maya testified that she has contacted the Marlboro police probably 40 or so times. David acknowledges that he has received probably 20 or so contacts from the police about complaints that the plaintiff has made to them."

I didn't say I received contacts, I just got reports that the police didn't bother to contact me about! They said they needed to file every report a woman asks for even if she says I came over with a flying saucer].

"And so it seems that it's not simply something that's new and really done for the purpose of keeping David from seeing the children."

The only two reports I had pursued were because I wasn't allowed to see my children when I went to pick them up for a court ordered visit!

"The plaintiff testified that the defendant has accessed personal papers, records, not really dealing with just the American Express card as Todd Prone argues, but also information concerning her sister and her sister's travel plans. Basically, he seems to have access to everything that the plaintiff does on her computer."

It is impossible to hack her computer with the firewall installed on it!

"The defendant acknowledged that he hired a private investigator to follow the plaintiff."

Curiously when Maya was confronted with this, she filed for the first restraining order out of the three attempts at this process!

"The defendant acknowledges that he showed up at her job, waiting outside. The plaintiff testified that she saw the defendant outside of the hospital just a month ago. She works at a hospital as a psychologist.
"The plaintiff, as I said before, has called the police a number of times because she has seen the defendant's car go by. I get the sense that the Marlboro police feel frustrated and don't have any concrete proof that these various things are occurring."

They do not have any proof. I wasn't in the vicinity of my house when most of these sets of allegations had supposedly happened, and the judge just said so!

"The plaintiff testified that her coworkers are asked by her consistently to walk her out to her car because she's fearful of what's going to happen. The plaintiff has testified that the defendant has pointed her out to strangers and she's concerned that this might be a way of identifying her to a stranger."

That happened in the child therapy office, and it was Vince!

"The plaintiff credibly testified that she believes the defendant is going to hurt her. She also testified that he has calculated her life insurance down to a penny, a number that she didn't even know.

"It sounds like things really came to a head on December the 29th last year. The defendant played a recording of an argument that took place and during that argument the plaintiff yelled 'I'll bury you,' but it sounded like she was more upset because the daughter was in the middle of the argument. It was disturbing that her daughter was present and privy to this argument."

Why is the Judge making up conclusions? The plaintiff is supposedly a psychologist, and our children suffer from Parental Alienation — that's a real disturbance!

"I can tell just by listening to the daughter's voice that she has heard and seen entirely too much. I'm sure that has negatively impacted her and no doubt it will continue to negatively impact her throughout her life unless she gets some assistance in dealing it.

"So the parties separated after that, I guess after the domestic violence issue, and they never resided together again."

After I found out she was having an affair!

"They've been going through the process with lawyers and with custody evaluations, and what have you. I suppose the burning question would be this: Why is the plaintiff here today?

"What motive does she have? Again, the defendant says the motive is the custody dispute."

And a very serious immigration issue — otherwise her temporary residence will be revoked, but the judge didn't allow this argument!

"I can't say that this would be her motive. I mean the custody dispute is proceeding before Judge Irish. Judge Irish will, I'm sure, listen very carefully to Dr. Psylie and any other people in the case. Apparently there was a Dr. Muller who is no longer involved because of a dispute, I suppose with the defendant.

"But I also heard the testimony not only of the plaintiff but also of her mother, Ingrid Getall, who was, I thought, a very credible witness. She cried when she testified that she truly believes that her daughter is in danger and that the defendant is a danger to her. She has been living with the plaintiff on and off for a period of eleven years.

"She testified very credibly that the defendant drives by, shouting out from the window. 'I'll kill you, Russian prostitute.'"

She speaks only Russian and I do not speak Russian and I assume that this Judge assumed that Ingrid Getall understands sign language, as this is the only language in which we could have had communication!

"That he has called the house occasionally and yelled all kinds of warnings and then hung up the phone. She believes it to be him. She doesn't know for sure.

"She said she last heard the defendant's voice on the phone in May of this year when he said her daughter is crazy and he's going to kill her, and called her a prostitute and a bitch and other bad words. She testified that the defendant has said these things in the presence of the children and indeed, she talked about the fact that the defendant would drive by as she was taking a walk with the children. She certainly has no real motive to lie, I mean, she loves her daughter."

So love of a daughter makes her a reliable witness? What about my love for my daughters? Did that count for nothing?

"Her testimony is mirrored very closely by what Maya was saying in her direct testimony. She outside in the hall when this testimony was given, so it's not something she was repeating."

The women live together and have been planning this for months! They don't need to hear each other's testimony!

"She testified that the defendant's car is white and the defendant acknowledged this. We also heard from the plaintiff's sister, Ilona Kissall. She testified that on or about November 3rd, the children were home when she answered the phone. She heard the defendant's voice saying that her 'bitch sister deserves to die.'"

A complete change from her original complaint!

"When her niece, Ally, picked up the phone, Ilona Kissall said she hung up. Apparently the daughter stayed on the phone and got so upset after the phone call that she called the police. This is evidenced by the police report marked P—2."

Ilona was the one who called the police and again pushes it on the innocent child!

"The police report says that a juvenile called to say her father's call to upset them. Now, again, it would have been more helpful if the police report was a little more detailed but you know, clearly the daughter made the call to 911. Ilona testified that the daughter started calling 911 before she even got upstairs. Ilona's testimony that the defendant threatened the plaintiff and the family many times and that the defendant calls the family in Ukraine is correct."

The family who understand no English!

"She also used the same word, saying that the defendant calls the plaintiff a prostitute. She said that she's also afraid for her sister's safety and well-being.

"I have found these witnesses to be credible. They testified to similar events even though, again, they didn't listen to each other's testimony. So I find that cumulatively all of this leads me to the inescapable conclusion that the defendant did contact the residence, even though his phone records don't seem to indicate that from his home phone or his cell phone he called the plaintiff's residence. I find that he did call the residence on or about November the 3rd of this year and that he did make this threat and that he did say, while the daughter remained on the phone, that something bad was going to happen. I do find that this incident did occur, just as testified. The plaintiff got the phone call at work. Her sister called her immediately at work and said, "Make sure somebody walks you out to your car." Why would she make that phone call if she wasn't afraid? "

Why is the judge making excuses for all these accusations?

"The plaintiff came to this court a few days later, that's true. But I find just as she testified, she works two jobs and the first available time that she could come to this court was on November the 6th. I don't find that she filed the restraining order as suggested by the defense in a knee-jerk reaction to receiving motion papers. Again, the custody battle has been ongoing for quite some time. And truly, I'm not going to get involved in modifying anything that's appearing before Judge Irish — that's his case. He'll decide the issues of custody and parenting time. My issue is, do I believe that the defendant uttered a terroristic threat on November the 3rd. The answer to that question is yes.

"A terroristic threat is defined at NJSA 2C:12—3. It said, basically, 'when one threatens to commit any crime of violence with the purpose to terrorize another.' The daughter got so upset that she immediately called the police. I find that the defendant has engaged in a course of conduct with the purpose of alarming and seriously annoying the plaintiff. Also that he has had the intention of harassing her in so doing. Again, it's true that when Maya came for one of her restraining orders, I believe I'm the one who denied it, telling her the denial was because she had just filed for a divorce and it's an upsetting time for everyone. That was in January of this year. To think that I'm having this discussion with these parties here in December of this year shows me that the level of anger has not diminished."

The fact was that the judge didn't understand that Maya needed this restraining order for immigration purposes and for my guaranteed removal from the marital home, and she had tried several times until she finally got one.

"I find that this is harassment pursuant to NJSA 2C:33—4. There is no other reason for her to be here really, other than her concern for her safety and well-being. Not only has she expressed it, but her mother and sister very credibly expressed it as well. As a result of all that has occurred, she's genuinely concerned. I'm sure Dr. Psylie and Dr. Muller and all the other therapists involved will advise Judge Irish and assist him in making his ultimate determination on the issues of custody and parenting time.

"I find it's necessary to issue a final restraining order in favor of the plaintiff because not only has she proved by a preponderance of the credible evidence the elements of terroristic threats and harassment, she has also proved to me that a final restraining order is necessary to protect her from immediate danger and to prevent further abuse under *Silver v. Silver*, 387, 112, an Appellate Division case from 2006.

"I'm going to go through this restraining order with you at this time. Just so you know, David, if there's a violation of the restraining order, it becomes a criminal contempt. If there's no violation of the restraining order, it's not a criminal matter; it's a civil matter. So it's extremely important that you listen carefully to the restraints I'm about to put in place.

"I'm going to bar you from going to the residence. What's that address?"

MAYA: "170 Memory Road, Marlboro, New Jersey 07746."

JUDGE: "So, do not go to 170 Memory Road, in Marlboro, New Jersey or, and I'm going to put in parentheses, within 1,000 feet of that residence. So do not even drive in that area. This way, if the mother is walking with the children, there will be no problem. Maya, I'm going to list your two places of employment. What are those?"

MAYA: "New Jersey Jail Forensic Center; it's the special treatment unit in the jail."

JUDGE: "Don't go to any of her work places. Maya, is there any other address I need to list?"

MAYA: "I don't know if it's possible, but could he be banned from coming to the places where my doctors are or any places I usually go to at specific times?"

JUDGE: "You also have Rusco Conservatory of Music. Can you put that down? Can you fit it in? Rusco Conservatory of Music in Red Bank. Does he use any of the same doctors or dentists as you do?

MAYA: "He's on my insurance."

JUDGE: "That's fine, but does he go to the same doctors?"

MAYA: "I changed my medical doctor, and I'm in the process of changing my dentist now."

JUDGE: "Okay. Well, I won't give him notice of which they are but obviously, if you see the plaintiff, David, you are to turn around and leave immediately. I'm going to prohibit you, David, from having any oral, written, personal, electronic or other form of contact or communication with the plaintiff, her sister, her mother, or any member of her family. David, this means you're not to have any contact or communication with the plaintiff, Ilona Kissall, Ingrid Getall and Ivan Ursol, do you understand?"

DAVID: "Yes your honor! I don't speak Russian or sign language, so I couldn't talk to most of them anyway. Also, except for the plaintiff, they don't even live in this country. I understand."

JUDGE: "I'm going to prohibit you from making or causing anyone else to make any harassing communications to the plaintiff or the others listed. I'm going to prohibit you from stalking, following, threatening to harm, etc. to the plaintiff or the others listed. I'm going to prohibit you from owning or possessing any weapons or firearms as well."

MAYA: "Your Honor, would you please include that he doesn't harass any of my coworkers or friends?"

DAVID: "Yes. All possible ways to block any real discovery of what she's really is where my assets have gone, as well as who she sleeps with nowadays when my children are left alone."

JUDGE: "Has he harassed any of your coworkers or friends recently?"

MAYA: "Yeah, my coworker. Can we just express that he cannot call my place of employment, as well as him not being allowed to go there?"

TODD: "Judge, may I raise an objection. I mean, there really has been no credible testimony that these people even received these phone calls that night."

JUDGE: "Well, I just think—"

TODD: "It's just another person in the loop, your honor, with all fairness that could call the police and make more allegations."

JUDGE: "Let me just say this to you, David. You should not call her places of employment. You should not call her coworkers or her friends. If she has to come in and say that you called her them, then you're going to have just another entity added. I won't add them today, but David, I'm telling you, do not call anyone associated with her. Do you understand?"

DAVID: "Your Honor, I never called them. She has called my office many times — I was let go from my last job because it. I constantly get threatening emails from her. Judge Irish has all the evidence and he didn't act on it. There is an issue now, and I'm going to lose my current job because of her constant harassment. I work for a major financial firm and I cannot have any type of police record. If I lose this job, I won't be able to pay child support and I'll be thrown into jail. She knows that and I assume she'll get satisfaction from it when it happens."

TODD: "David, listen to the Judge."

DAVID: "Filing of this Final Restraining Order will destroy me as an honest, record-free hard-working citizen of this country. I feel that I could receive a more just trial in the Soviet Union than I've had here. It is sad for my children, for my family and for this nation as a whole that things like this go on. I'll never be able to get a paying responsible job again after this. My professional class will be shifted down to where all I can do is flip burgers for a living! Everything I make will then go to child support and a woman who makes more than me."

TODD: "David, listen to the Judge."

DAVID: "That's one of the motives behind this action. I don't know what I can do about it, but this court is hers. I'm considered an abuser by the law and immigration, and by this government, all based on an *alleged* phone call that was never made, and all of this happened 11 months *after* I left my home and contact with my children!"

JUDGE: "Okay. Now, as far as parenting time, we're referencing the FM. There's not a pending weapons case? Lorie, there's not a pending weapons case? All right, is there anything else I need to address in this order for your safety and protection, Maya?"

MAYA: "No, I think we addressed everything."

JUDGE: "Now, I have to impose a domestic violence victim's fund fine. This fine can range up to $500. I'll impose a $100 fine payable within 30 days. If there are any further problems, Maya, then you should notify the police."

MAYA: "Okay."

JUDGE: "I'm going to hand down these papers to each of you; this goes to the plaintiff and this to the defendant. Now, David, please take a seat in the front row. My staff will take you to the Sheriff's Department to be fingerprinted so that you can't obtain a firearm."

MAYA: "Thank you so much, your honor."

TODD: "Thank you."

JUDGE: "Thank you, Todd Prone."

DAVID: "Your honor, I just want to let you know that you've just destroyed a man with your decision. A decision made with perjured testimony! I guess I have to live with the fact that my children will never have a father, and that fault lies with you."

TODD: "David, I'll talk to you outside."

DAVID: "I applied for custody and I'm not going to get it. That's another motive for this Final Restraining Order, in addition to the immigration motive that the court didn't allow. I've been framed in this land of democracy."

JUDGE: "I understand your argument."

DAVID: "I'm going to lose my job because of this, and now she can have complete custody, get the marital home and become a citizen of this country, bypassing all immigration laws. Where is justice? How could it be so blind?"

TODD: "David?"

DAVID: "I brought up the immigration issue because this woman was on the verge of being deported when I married her. The plaintiff is a woman who came to this country illegally, got married in order to get every tangible thing I worked for, and now takes away my dignity, my assets and my children. She has made a mockery of the legal system by using the VAWA laws created to protect women who are really in need."

TODD: "The Judge just ordered—"

JUDGE: "David?"

DAVID: "By this decision my professional future is over and I'm dismissed from my work.

TODD: "I'll talk to you outside, David."

DAVID: "She's a user. She used me and now she's used the legal system."

JUDGE: "Talk to your attorney outside. He'll discuss the matter with you."

Outside the courtroom, I looked at my counsel and asked, "Why has this legal system forsaken me for a bunch of lies? Why didn't the Judge see the truth? I thought judges were skilled at seeing through lies."

Todd Prone looked at me with pity. "The case was lost the moment the Judge came out of her chambers. She made up her mind just going over all the police reports."

"What do you mean?" I asked nervously.

"There was a preponderance of former evidence in the eyes of the court. All the previous attempts to get restraining orders and the dozens of police reports sealed your case."

I thought about this for a moment, as Todd's words settled in my mind. The police reports didn't have any merit. Any person can file dozens of them without any basis in reality. However, I finally got it. It was a fix. "The hearing lasted for two hours just so the Judge could affirm her predisposed decision?"

"Yes, that's the way it seems. She denied every objection I raised." Todd turned around and seemed to be in a hurry to get to his next appointment.

This day the nightmares of worry about whether I should have lawyer and what would happen with the restraining order ended in an astounding defeat. The truth didn't prevail, and I was out the $3,000 that went to a counsel who did a lousy job of representing me — just as Vince had predicted. Now I knew what it felt like to be a victim of the legal system, the family court, and the greedy sharks swimming in cash around the misery generated by this legal system.

I came to an inescapable conclusion — everything is business and money! The paraphernalia of the law generated business and didn't necessary create or keep the order of the law. Take for example, our lucrative prison systems, where the taxpayer spends an average of $50,000 a year on incarcerated non-violent offenders, when that amount could pay for treatment, housing and an education! I realized that we cannot feel truly secure under our umbrella of civilized society.

How many prisoners are locked up because of a Judge's unfair decisions or prejudice? I wondered, as I was led away by the court officer to a special room where I was fingerprinted and photographed. I realized that from this point forward I would have a criminal record that would show up on every background check, every arrival on international flights and traffic stops. I was now condemned to being treated differently by police officers everywhere in the USA. I'd stopped being a truly free man.

A week later, because of this, I had to leave my high-paying job, and became an IT consultant, seeking any short-term contracts that were available, albeit with very low pay.

CHAPTER EIGHTEEN

The Arrest

I was on the way home, after my long commute back from NYC during a bitterly cold evening. I was walking slowly to avoid slipping on snow that was quickly turning into ice. I had slipped before and the painful experience forced me to slow down, even while I was trying to hurry home from the train station.

I was walking towards my apartment in the Exelon Complex in Aberdeen NJ. I lived in an apartment on the third floor of a four-story complex that looked more like a fancy hotel than an apartment building. It had all the amenities of an average hotel, too.

When I finally reached my apartment complex, I saw a police cruiser with all its lights flashing. This temporarily blinded me, but after a second or two my eyes adjusted. I could see two officers seated in the car, and one of them scanning me with his flashlight.

I was shocked, but walked quietly toward the police cruiser. The moment I reached it, both doors opened simultaneously and the two officers emerged while the engine was still running. One officer was tall and then and the other one was short and heavy; both had serious, scary looks on their faces.

"Mr. Tal?"

"Yes, that's me."

"Please come with us," the tall officer said as he reached out for my left arm and gripped it tightly. He then forcefully directed me to the back seat of the police cruiser.

"We just need to question you. Your wife said that you were seen again near her home and you tried to enter the home against the restraining order."

"Are you serious?"

"Yes. We have to take you in and you'll be brought in front of a judge."

"It's not true! I'll lose my job. I'll be barred from any finance-related jobs forever if I have an arrest record in addition to the restraining order."

"We'll have to lock you up for 12 hours, until someone posts bail for you, or you stand before a judge."

"If you really didn't do this, the Judge will release you and we won't keep you locked up, sir," he declared, confidently.

"'I don't understand," I said, shrugging my shoulders. "How I can be arrested based solely on what my spouse is saying? How can I continue living this way? This isn't justice! You're police officers, don't you see that this allegation isn't true?"

"We're only doing our jobs and serving the law. You can contact your lawyer. The system isn't rocket science for any lawyer."

We approached the county jail and the standard red tape procedure began. The place smelled like a jail and I felt humiliated just being there.

"Don't leave me here, officers. Can I stay with you for a while until I call my friend? I don't have a lawyer now; I represent myself."

"Get a lawyer or other help and then arrange for someone to post bail for you. What is it exactly that you're frightened of?" the officer asked.

"I'm afraid of being here. I'm a law-abiding citizen and a professional. I've never been in Jail. This isn't a place I ever thought I would be. I'm a thinker, not a criminal."

What really frightened me was the mechanical and routine way the police handled the arrest and my delivery to the county jail. I realized that they do the same thing to dozens of men on a weekly basis. It was a fact of life for them. I knew right from wrong and finally realized that my life choices had brought me to this point. I was going to be imprisoned, even though I was innocent.

I looked intently, without blinking, at my new accommodations. I had always thought of a prison as a place where every man banished from society for violating the laws of society deserved to be. I thought only specific people from the edge of society were put there. Here, in this county jail I saw people from all walks of life, every nationality, race and religion, all jammed in together. I wondered what their stories were.

My arms and legs started to quiver like those of a man afflicted with some kind of sickness, as I imagined the horrors and agonies each one of these men might have endured or caused others to endure. Johnny the county jail policeman, a sturdy, well-rounded, brown-haired man with a full round face and big red cheeks, sat across a metal desk and as he talked with me he swayed to and fro and from time to time glanced at the TV screen at the opposite end of the room, viewing a basketball game. He was supposed to register me and take me to my cell, which I would share with dozens of other people. I tried to ease my tension by whistling, but that earned me a dirty look from policeman Johnny.

"You'll be locked up here until you see a judge tomorrow or until someone posts a bail for you," Johnny asserted briefly. "You'll need to surrender all of your personal belongings and change into these clothes," he said, addressing me with a stern commanding voice, while handing me a beige uniform of sweat pants and a shirt that looked more like something I would wear for a nightly run.

Faint with the horror of the situation, I looked back and thanked the officer. He then pointed to a brightly lit corner room, which was close to his location behind the reception desk. The room had no doors. While walking to the room, inquisitive eyes were looking at me from all directions. I ignored them and changed my clothes, then the officer led me to the cell while every inmate watched with interest. When the officer locked me in, a murmur that sounded like a faint "hi" passed through the crowd and I waved to everyone.

"I've done nothing … I'm here because of my venomous wife," I told the crowd.

A bunch of mumbled responses surrounded me and all of them were shaking their heads with understanding. They probably heard the same statement of innocence with every new inmate.

I sat down over the edge of my bed and the inmate whose bed was across from me started a conversation. It seemed like he was just trying to cheer me up.

"It seems that your case is similar to mine. I'm here because of a restraining order violation brought up by my ex-wife, too. However, I'm ready ... I have full confidence in this legal system and the way the law is served ... and I entrust my fate to this system."

As I heard my cellmate declare that he trusted his fate to the system, I froze and turned toward him. "What if the judge declares you guilty?"

The man's composure changed and he turned a dreadful look towards me, while some shouts of agreement sounding like sinister echoes came from the people who overheard our conversation. The man was unhappy, as he had just been trying to cheer me up and I had thrown reality back into his face.

The lights were turned off and we heard the main door slamming closed. There was a swish of a whisper that sounded like "good night" from my neighbor and I responded with a faint response. I began to get tired and there was a dull ache in my stomach while my head was throbbing. For some time several persons were still talking in the cell; however, their conversation couldn't stop me entering into a deep sleep. After all, it wasn't the first time I had slept in the company of men. I was once a soldier and I was trained to sleep under all sorts of conditions.

My good friend, Vince, came to the court the next morning and arranged bail as soon as he could, and I was again a free man. The coming Friday, I was invited to a party on Long Island and the following Thursday, April 18, was my birthday. I really wanted to be free of this episode by that time, as I was planning to see my children on my birthday.

CHAPTER NINETEEN

The Love Party

It was Friday evening and it was snowing lightly. The trees were covered with snow and it was beautiful driving through them along the local roads as I viewed the big manicured houses in Upper Brookville, Long Island. I arrived at the house where the "Love Party" was taking place. I was surprised to see the well-maintained circular driveway and the beautiful front yard with a large white stucco house behind it. This was the party that the husband of a former Ms. Universe was throwing to celebrate his dedicated love for his wife. My car was taken away by the valet and I walked toward the big door. The organizer of the party asked me, "You're Mr. Tal, aren't you?"

"How do you know?" I asked timidly.

"My friend Katherine once met you, and you look exactly as she described," she said, then she led me to a seat next to Katherine.

Katherine was a recent divorcee with piercing blue eyes, who was blond, slim and tall. I had met her only once before at one of the social events I attended several months ago. From my conversation with her the last time we met, she seemed slightly confused about her identity — her mother was Jewish American and her father was Catholic Irish American. These facts were revealed through conversations I had with her discussing my two little daughters, who also were of mixed religions.

"I'm glad to see you again," as Katherine rose from her seat and shook my hands. She was several inches taller than me. Suddenly she gave me a tight hug that lasted too long for my taste and I found it peculiar.

"I'm also glad to see *you* again!" Katherine responded warmly. "How is your divorce going?"

"I still have problems with visitation. A man really needs to be persistent and strong in this battle over the love of his children. Sometimes I wonder if I'll have to give up seeing my children, just like so many men in this country have had to do."

"Do not give up!" Katherine responded as I glanced at her sweet, sensitive face.

"Don't worry. I'll never give up my children. I'll overcome all obstacles to establish my parental rights!"

Katherine just smiled back, but her smile had a hint of mistrust and bitterness. There was something about this that made me assume right away that she had experienced something similar.

"Are you a single mother?" I asked daringly, knowing that this was a question that should not be asked in this circumstance.

Katherine's bustling expression of self-confidence changed and she turned towards me, bringing her eyes close to my face. "Yes, I am," she answered gently.

I was attracted to her and thought that I could fall in love with her one day, if the sickness ravaging my body by some miracle disappeared by a miracle. That sweet thought was replaced with mistrust. *What if she's doing the same to her ex-husband? What if she doesn't let her husband see his child?*

"My ex-husband left me for another woman before delivery of his child, and he isn't interested in seeing him. He's not made of the same stuff as you," she explained sadly.

I looked at Katherine like I didn't understand her response. "I'll see you around. I'm going to get a drink," I said. I started walking toward the dining room and then I walked though a corridor connecting the kitchen and the dining room.

Suddenly it felt like two hands were gripping me from behind. I turned around and held my stomach with both hands, as the sharp pain wracked my body. Definitely the cancer was there and I could feel it now.

"What's wrong?" I heard Katharine asking as she approached me. She said with a slightly drunk and heavily pronounced voice, "I find men with humor to be very sexy!" She then proceeded to kiss me in a displeasing way.

There's no way out! I thought, knowing that my rejection of this slightly drunk woman could cost me the possibility of a future relationship with her. I gently pushed Katherine away and said, "Katherine, not now, not this way and not today!"

Katherine raised her voice with slight anger noticeable in her high-pitched response, "So, you do not want my love?"

There was no doubt that Katherine was inebriated, so I said nothing. I returned to my place at the table and just sank down. I put my hands on the table and gazed at Katherine, who chose to stand next to the door leading into the corridor. She returned my gaze with a look of dismay, her eyes burning with unmistakable signs of anger.

I suddenly flashed back to my divorce process and then to my military experience. I remembered that I was about a mile behind an enemy MIG and I was ready to send the second missile away.

> *"Hey, I'm gonna get you too.*
> *Another one bites the dust"*
> *I selected the missile and squeezed the trigger.*
> *"How do you think I'm going to get along,*
> *Without you, when you're gone*
> *You took me for everything that I had,*
> *And kicked me out on my own."*

The MIG exploded into a red, blue, silver and black ball of fire and debris, and I performed a steep climbing turn to the right to avoid hitting the debris. I looked out through the clear glass cockpit and the sky was full of maneuvering jets, and I could see one spiraling to the ground. *Thank God it was a MIG*, I thought to myself.

I suddenly woke up from my flashback, and found myself staring at Katherine, with a strong realization that in war or any conflict eventually there are no winners. I approached Katherine, shook her hand and gave her a kiss on her cheek. "I hope we will meet again. I have to leave now."

"I hope you will see me again!" she responded with a husky strong voice. Confirming that she was completely drunk.

After I left the party, I found out the real story behind this "love party." The couple were recently married and celebrating their union. The hostess had been Miss Universe over 30 years ago and her husband of the last 25 years had died recently. The host of the party, a known and established psychiatrist, had been in love with her since high school and had divorced his wife in order to marry this woman. Love has many angles.

CHAPTER TWENTY

Maya and Dr. Rosensthal

On the morning of April 18, Maya was rushing to meet her mentor, Dr. Rosensthal. After sending me away she drove her children to school and rushed to meet Dr. Rosensthal all the way to Hagway hospital. The hospital was nested on a mountaintop in a country-like area of western New Jersey that looked like a resort area, and didn't look like a psychiatric hospital.

Dr. Rosensthal's office was in the main campus, which was a fixture in that area and visible from afar. The building had a façade that displayed decorated white stone and it was three stories high. Dr. Rosensthal was about 64 years old, about 5'6" tall and had short white hair and a white trimmed beard. He was suffering from the onset of Parkinson disease and his left hand quivered constantly.

On that morning, Maya was elated that she was going to meet Dr. Rosensthal. It seemed as though she got her batteries charged when she met him, and she seemed to gain a lot of knowledge, connections and confidence from her relationship with him. Maya was ready to drive the 75 miles just to spend less than an hour with his conversation and guidance.

She was supposed to meet Dr. Rosensthal at 9 a.m. and was late because of heavy traffic on that sunny morning. She arrived at Hagway at 9:30 a.m. and entered the lobby at the main campus. Her thoughts were distracted and she didn't bother to put her name on the security guest list. The security guard called her back, but she ignored his call and ran to Dr. Rosensthal's office.

His was a mid-sized office, painted in standard white, with two large windows with a view of the beautiful valley that begins about 100 yards from the hospital. The view and windows were a sign of status in this hospital and Dr. Rosensthal earned this status after 25 years of service.

The office was decorated with Rosenthal's diplomas and certificates, and books on different subjects of psychology filled a tall bookcase running the whole length of the office. There was always a coffee pot filled with freshly brewed coffee, and CNN was the channel of choice on the television that was on when he wasn't a seeing patient. His desk was covered with files and he was reviewing one of them.

"Sorry I'm late!"

"It is okay, my young friend," he answered. "How is your husband?"

"He's fine. He just came this morning to see his children. I was going to call the police and he left," Maya answered.

"You know I was going over your background files and you didn't tell me you were an abused child."

"I wasn't," Maya answered assertively.

"I see in the file a note that you wrote stating that your father hit your mother and caused her to abort."

"Who gave you that note?"

"David submitted all his notes, emails and documentation regarding you and your internship in this hospital. Yesterday he sent me the last batch of documents," Dr. Rosensthal answered. "I see also from his notes that you had a trauma when your father left. You were thirteen years old then."

"Yes, it was a traumatic experience," Maya answered.

Dr. Rosensthal started reading one of the documents aloud, "I never knew that people could have so much hatred for each other and could so easily forget all those years they spent together. My father left, and for a number of years didn't really care how we lived. He somehow forgot that he had children. Did you write that?"

"Yes, I did," Maya answered.

"David also said that your mother used to physically abuse you."

"She just hit me sometimes," Maya responded.

"Did she force you to marry young so she could get you out of the house?"

"She didn't force me, but it was understood," Maya answered.

"You know, the stories you told me about David being abusive to you just don't make sense," Dr. Rosensthal said.

"Why?"

"Because, David came from a stable loving home and this was what he was trying to give you."

"But he abused me!" Maya yelled.

"He did write that he believed in marriage, love and children as his principles and as a foundation for a strong society. He also stated that he'd go to great lengths to have his relations with his children restored. He also mentioned that he learned the psychological consequences when children lose a loving bond with a parent. He said that he hopes you also understand that too.

"I talked with you about attachment theory many times. Don't you remember? You came from an abusive home. You have the tools to understand the effects and take treatment to eliminate the them," Dr. Rosensthal said quietly, staring directly into Maya's eyes.

"David knew your background and tried to help you in every way. He also backed you financially in your academic pursuits as you worked toward your PhD in psychology. I know he helped you with every assignment and document you wrote, he paid for all your spending sprees and also your tuition, because he loved you and hoped you would learn to understand yourself."

"I'm not sure what you're saying, Dr. Rosensthal. Don't you understand that he was the abusive spouse in this relationship?"

"No, *you* were! The only proof of abuse I have is a suggested threatening phone call, for which because of your complaint, you got an order of protection. In all the police reports David has mailed me there is no proof of any of your accusations. They were all figments of your imagination!" Dr. Rosensthal yelled back.

"In his notes he mentioned that you used to yell at him, mock him, call him names, and make derogatory remarks about his ethnicity and virility," Dr. Rosenthal continued. "I hope this isn't true," he added.

"He also said that you used to go out at night, saying you didn't need to tell him where you were going, and that you used to come back after midnight." Is this true?" Dr. Rosensthal asked and angrily.

Maya just sat there with a grim face and didn't answer. She had started to realize what was happening.

"David reported symptoms such as tightness in the stomach, muscular pain, racing pulse, thought distortion, and panic attacks, and you did nothing. These are psychosomatic symptoms of abuse. You're a psychologist; you were my protégé, you were my favorite student. Don't you see what you've done?" Dr. Rosensthal asked with a tinge of contempt. "You didn't hesitate to make false allegations of violence to achieve your goal!"

"I do not know what you're talking about and you're not blameless in this situation," Maya accused. "You slept with me several times when I was supposedly your interring student, while at the same time you said you were happily married."

"Don't preach at me, I know you used me while you were having your real affair with Dr. Brown. I know exactly what you are!" he answered.

Suddenly the TV volume seemed to increase and the announcer announced: "Breaking news. This just in…" The screen turned blue for a second and Dr. Rosensthal turned toward the TV to see what had happened. "A small plane has just crashed in a parking lot in New Jersey. We await further information and will interrupt regular programming as we get more information."

Dr. Rosensthal turned back and continued his conversation with Maya and asked, "Do you know that despair is usually the result of male abuse, the fact that there is no other option and a strong sense of powerlessness which often leads men to intense emotional pain and feelings about death?"

"I really don't care much about David or how he feels. He was just a stepping stone for me," Maya responded.

"Why didn't I see this sooner," Dr. Rosensthal wondered aloud.

"You were a stepping stone too. I used you to get a job and build professional contacts. You used me as well, to boost your ego by having sex with a younger woman." Maya replied in a heated and angry manner.

"You're wrong!" Dr. Rosensthal yelled back.

"You'd better get your story straight, doctor. I have enough evidence to show that you slept with me. I learned from Monika Lewinski how to keep such evidence," Maya screamed back at him.

"You're a psychopath!" Dr. Rosensthal shouted and then his body went into spasm as though he was having a seizure.

Maya ignored his distress and started arranging her bag. She was ready to leave.

Again the TV volume seemed to increase and the announcer announced: "We have further information regarding the plane crash in New Jersey. The private plane crashed in a parking lot near a house in Marlboro, NJ. One person was killed, the pilot, who was apparently alone in the craft when it went down." Scenes of the crash flashed on the screen, and Maya just stood there as though lightning had struck her.

"That's near my house!" she exclaimed.

"You may not have a husband to worry about now!" Dr. Rosensthal yelled sarcastically.

"You're crazy. We need to coordinate our stories," Maya said.

Dr. Rosensthal opened his drawer and took out a Walter PPK. Maya looked at him with dismay.

"I have advanced glioblastoma multiforme — brain cancer — and I have nothing to lose. This was your husband's favorite service gun. Wasn't it?" Dr. Rosensthal asked while waving the weapon in her face.

Maya was stunned. "Why are you pointing that gun at me?" Maya then asked fearfully.

"Because you have ruined 30 years of my career," Dr. Rosensthal answered.

"You and I helped kill a man, how can we continue in this profession? I'm ruined. David sent the files to me but he probably also sent them to the police."

"We're not involved. We see dozens of patients who do kill themselves and I'll not take the blame for this," Maya answered.

"No, he had cancer too. He only had weeks to live. You caused him to take this extreme route and I helped it happen," Dr. Rosensthal said quietly. "David sent me documents with copies of our e-mail correspondence. He also sent session notes of our attitudes and jokes about some of your patients who committed suicide. There was a specific incriminating note that said that you wished a patient of yours would commit suicide, and I responded callously. There was another specific e-mail where you joked about the patient's mental status and his progressive disease, and my 'funny' cruel responses were noted in this e-mail.

"Do you remember the e-mail exchange we had about your patient, Mr. Smith?"

"Yes, he's the guy with MS who said he wanted to committed suicide," Maya said. "You said it would be a relief for you and probably his family, too. I remember many funny emails about that. I think you even said that you couldn't wait for him to execute his plan."

"You said, I hope he'll carry out his threats, that lunatic," Dr. Rosenthal said, "and he did it the next day. What type of professionals are we? A tumor is ending my life and this will end my career. This is how I'll be remembered. David has exposed us. I won't be able to show my face in this hospital ever again!

Dr. Rosensthal took the gun and aimed it at his forehead.

"And you, Maya, you're going to live a long life, but your career in psychology has ended almost before it began!"

Maya took her bag and ran out, her skirt flying in the wind and revealing her long legs. She had something white dripping from the edges of her mouth. She was screaming, "Help! Help!" but it sounded more like a person having a stroke. No one paid much attention, probably assuming she was a patient who perhaps hadn't taken her medication.

Maya started running towards her car, but one of the security guards ran after her and stopped her. "What wing did you run away from?" he asked

"I'm a doctor of psychology," Maya replied

"Me, too," the guard replied with a smirk. The guard then pulled Maya's arms behind her and tried to cuff her like any other violent patient in the hospital.

Maya again yelled, "I'm a doctor! I'm a doctor! I'm a doctor!"

Suddenly Maya heard a voice in her head that whispered, "Not anymore."

"Is it you, Dr. Rosensthal? Why did you do this? "Maya screamed. "What have I done, what have I done?" By this point she was crying hysterically.

"You did wrong," the voice said.

The guard handcuffed Maya and called for help using his hand-held radio. "I have a patient here who needs immediate attention!" he shouted into the microphone.

Police sirens were heard and several police cars arrived. The guard led Maya to the first police cruiser and opened the door. When Maya saw the police officers approaching, she seemed to regain her sanity and quietly asked the guard to look in her purse for her credentials. Maya knew how to act when dealing with the police — she'd done it many times when she'd called them to the house when she was trying to get David removed.

The guard dug out Maya's IDs and presented them to the officers. One of them removed the handcuffs from her wrists, and led her to the chief investigator.

"David? David, please come and help me," Maya whispered.

The chief investigator asked the officer to verify Maya's credentials and then asked her to sit down. "We know the whole story," he said

"What story?"

"We know the reasons for everything that's happened. We got the files from your husband, David, this morning. I've been on the phone with the Marlboro police regarding this case. Now I understand why the files were sent to my attention, even though I'm 75 miles away from Marlboro."

"How do you know?" Maya asked

"Two people died today and at this time we can't do anything," the chief said. "We won't hold you but we will need to question you further at a later time."

Maya got up, picked up her handbag and was ready to leave. "Thank you officer," she said and smiled. She then turned and walked slowly towards her car.

"She doesn't understand what's happened or she doesn't have the morality to understand, but I *do* know she's in the wrong profession. Hopefully God will punish her one day," the chief thought as he watched her walk way.

CHAPTER TWENTY-ONE

Ally's Inheritance

Five years later, on April 18 in one of the middle class apartment buildings in Elizabeth, New Jersey, a young girl sat at the window of Apartment 10A, staring down at the street below. The girl, Ally, was a thin and graceful little brunette. She was five feet, five inches tall with sad looking brown eyes. She waved to the mailman who was standing below.

Ally was a really beautiful young girl, with a light olive complexion and beautiful big brown eyes. Her smile showed dazzling white teeth, and she smiled often, but the smile didn't always reach her eyes. There was something a bit melancholy about her.

The mailman had delivered letters to this building for the last several years and knew Ally. Several minutes later, the mailman knocked on the door of Apartment 10A. Ally, now a post high-school student on her way to her first college year, looked through the peephole and observed the mailman, who held a large envelope. He waved the parcel when he noticed her looking at him. His face was shiny with perspiration and he was out of breath from climbing the three flights of stairs to get there.

"You have a package from Ms. Tal," the mailman said.

"Wait a second; I'm trying to get the locks open!" Ally said, as she finally opened the door and greeted the mailman. "Thanks coming all the way up just to deliver this package."

"That's my job," he answered and handed over the package.

"Have a good day, Ally!" he said in a friendly tone as he turned back toward the stairs.

After she closed and locked the door, Ally walked toward the kitchen to get a knife so she could open the package. She turned her head upwards and looked at the ceiling as though she was praying. "I wonder why grandma is sending a package now. She normally only sends birthday cards and a few letters." she mumbled to herself as she walked.

Ally ripped the package open in one swift movement and took out the contents, which she then spread across the kitchen table. Ally was surprised to see page after page of printed material. Suddenly she was excited. She knew the contents had belonged to her long-dead father. After a few moments of contemplation, she picked up the first letter, which was addressed to her and was from her grandmother.

> *Dear Ally,*
>
> *I promised my son I'd send you this package when you turned 18. My health is not good, and I wanted to give it to you while I was still able to answer your questions. I know you're mature and strong enough to handle this information now. These are your dad's personal letters and legal materials concerning his divorce from your mother, he also included notes on why he left you and your sister.*
>
> *Please don't read the material I've marked with a red marker until you reach the age of 21, as I'm sure they may cause you some discomfort with regard to what happened to your dad.*
>
> *Please know that your dad loved you and Anika more than anything in this world.*
>
> *Love,*
> *Grandmother*

Ally started sifting through the material. She picked up one letter and shivered as she recognized her dad's handwriting.

Dear Ally,

I hope the material here won't upset you, but you need to know the truth about what happened. Please remember me as I was when you were young. I know that what happened between your mother and me left scars you will carry all your life, but you have to know that your mother and I both love you, even though we cannot live together.

I will always love you and Anika and I'll watch over you forever.

Love,
Dad

Ally continued sifting through the papers, reading them selectively. She found some of the letters her father had sent to her mother, pledging to give her an amicable divorce. Ally also found out that her father was terminally ill before he died, and she was surprised. That wasn't what her mother had told her.

"It's all clear to me now," she said out loud. "Father did love us. He didn't cause all the problems like mother led us to believe."

In the last several years of their wanderings from one apartment to another after they had left the house in Marlboro, Ally had tried to get in touch with several of her friends from the old neighborhood. Now that they had all finished high school, each had moved on to a new circle of friends, and probably some of them had completely forgotten her.

One of them, Jennifer, was still living in the old neighborhood and infrequently corresponded with Ally through emails. Jennifer's father knew Ally's father when they lived in Marlboro, and Ally decided to contact her.

Jennifer, who was her friend from early childhood times, was a clever and interesting girl who wished to study the Greek heritage of her mother's native land. She played the guitar and liked music. Ally remembered that her father and Jennifer's father used to talk quite often while they visited each other's homes. Jennifer's father had previously been married before and after that divorce, he was never able to see his daughter again. He was bitter about this, and used to discuss it in detail.

Ally texted her friend and told her she needed to understood what had happened to her father. Jennifer immediately called her.

"Hi Jennifer, what's new?"

"Hi Ally, long time—"

"I've just read some documents my father left me. After reading them and his letters I need some help to understand what really happened with him. Do you think your father would talk to me? He seemed to know my father pretty well."

"Sure, Ally. I'll ask him to call you when he's back from work."

Later that evening, Ally sat down on the sofa and began thinking about the events of the day. She fell into a restless asleep, and woke an hour later when the telephone rang. Ally jumped off the sofa, and ran toward the telephone.

"Hi, Ally, this is Mark, Jennifer's dad. She told me about the documents from your father."

"Hi, Mark, it's good talking with you again," Ally said.

"Jennifer said you wanted to understand what happened. I know he had to struggle through the difficulties unfairly imposed on him by your mother. He discussed it with me because we were in similar situations. I couldn't ever see my daughter again because of my divorce, and your father was facing the same future with you and your sister. My wife was similar to your mother, too. Any time I tried to see my daughter, she'd call the police."

"I wasn't able to withstand the long court battle needed in order to see my daughter. Eventually, I moved out of state, remarried and started my over. For me, my daughter is as good as dead since I'll never see her again.

"Your father fought to the bitter end for the right to see you again. He fought like a real soldier. I would never have been able to continue the battle like he did. He was repeatedly in court for one main reason — to regain visitation rights. He wanted to be sure the divorce didn't cause any psychological damage to you and Anika.

"He lost his life savings in the battle, due to high legal fees and lawyers who took advantage of your mother's animosity and anger towards your father. I remember that he once told me that he refused to accept any Judge's decision denying him custody and that he would not be joining the majority of American fathers who never see their children again."

"I told your father about all my troubles and that's why he came to me when his own issues began. He knew I'd understand what he was going through. "Mark, I'm terribly sorry to hear your point of view of what happened to you, but it did help me understand my father."

"Of course! I told your father that, and that's why he came to me — because he knew I'd' understand. The whole process was debilitating for me — I'm on my third heart attack and my health problems started with my battles with the legal system. The stress is detrimental to many people who go through this process. Apparently your father was no exception. Jennifer told me that your father was terminally ill before his death."

"Yes, he had pancreatic cancer."

"I'm sorry to here that. He was a great guy."

"I'm going to have to hang up now, Mark, but this conversation was extremely helpful."

"Read your father's letters carefully, Ally. Let me know if there's anything else I can help you with."

"Bye, Mark and thanks again for your time"

Ally now understood that her parents' marriage had never been wasn't the paradise of two lovers turned into disaster. She suspected it was more a financial stepping-stone for her mother where she and Anika were the ultimate losers. Ally her father saying, "Divorce is a declaration of war between two people. The children will always be the losers of this emotional war, while lawyers and other professionals profit from it." She understood it much better now.

Ally heard the front door open and she saw her mother, Maya, coming in. She was dressed in black high-heeled shoes with pointy toes and a flimsy white dress through which her long bare legs and their distinctive varicose veins visible. An ID tag for the prison where she worked hung from her belt. She looked tired and worn out; the years of double shifts and long hours in a prison environment had taken their toll.

"Where's Anika?" Maya asked.

"She went to sleep early," Ally said. "I've been reading all the material Dad sent to me."

Maya stood frozen in shock for a few seconds, then asked in a menacing voice, "What material? How did you get it?"

Ally stepped back in fear, her breathing escalated, and said nothing.

"What material were you reading?" Maya asked again impatiently.

Ally's hand reached over and grasped some of the papers from the packet. "These are some of Dad's notes that he had my grandmother keep for me. She mailed them to me and I got them today. I've read every letter and document in this packet."

"Why are you reading this material? Are you going on with that crazy nonsense about your dad? Haven't you given up his memory yet?" Maya yelled

"The truth is here! What I found out about my dad isn't much different than what I'd always thought. I knew my memories of him were correct. You've tried so hard all these years to make Anika and me believe he was a bad man, when the opposite was true. Why didn't you tell us the truth? I'm so angry with you right now!"

"Wait, Ally. You don't understand. I can't tell you how scary your father really was. It was as though he was possessed by the devil, and it drove him to his death! I know your grandmother just sent that stuff to ruin my relationship with you."

"But all this material isn't made up. Look at this document; this is his handwriting! I remember Dad's handwriting — it was distinctive. Look at all the documents and letters; they're real. You wanted us to grow up without a father just like you did. I know the pain of growing up without a father, but you added to it by trying to make us hate our father. You tainted our memories of him!"

"Ally, have you lost your mind?" asked Maya. "I won't stand for you talking that way to me!"

"Oh, Mother, please. I see the truth now. You don't understand what I'm feeling right now. It doesn't mean anything to you! Anika and I have been here with you for years and we've never heard a single *true* word about what really happened!"

Maya yawned and looked disinterested. She nonchalantly filled the coffee pot with water and put it on the stove. "Ally," Maya went on after she'd finished with the pot, "the great time I can't believe you'd even want me to talk about your father."

"Come on, Mother. Why did you besmirch our father's memory? Why did you let us grow up with distorted views about him? You're a psychologist and I assume you know that children need also their father. Not having him around can affect them psychologically. It is called the attachment theory, isn't it? I read about this theory in one of the articles you wrote. I can barely look at you right now!"

Maya turned towards Ally with an intense look of disdain. Her glare insinuated violence. Ally realized that there was no way getting out of this awkward situation, so she approached Maya and tried to hug her.

"Mother, I'll always love you but you have to realize that what you've done to us is not right!"

Maya deliberately looked up toward the ceiling and pushed Ally away. Then she glared at the pile of documents on the table with a look of intense disgust. "Don't you see? Your father is doing it to us again, this time from the grave!" Maya said evilly. "I had to keep him away from you."

Ally jumped up and raised her hands with anger and startled Maya, who moved back a step.

"You don't get it, Mother. We *needed* our father. We didn't want to go through childhood without a father who cared for us and loved us. We didn't want to be like you!" Ally defiantly.

There was a look of distress and anguish on Maya's face. She closed her eyes for a moment and sighed, then babbled something unintelligible in Russian. "What a pity that your outlook has changed," she said finally. "I thought I was your only parent forever. I took care of you, fed you and nurtured you. Just ignore that pile of documents, I beg you. They will only causes a rift between us."

"Oh, save it, Mother! I'm tired of your lies. I needed my father. I have good memories of him and I feel horrible guilt for having suppressed them for so long. I plan to read through all of his documents again so I can know him better."

Maya uttered strange sounds that seemed like the angry growl of a wounded animal, then said "Ally, I do not understand!"

"What don't you understand? I learned the truth today. Just go away, Mother. I'll talk with you tomorrow. I have some decisions to make. Please leave me alone!"

Maya stomped off toward her bedroom door and before slamming the door shut, she muttered, "My daughter raised her voice to me. There's no denying, it was an angry voice."

"She doesn't understand!" Maya muttered to herself once she was alone. "Well, what am I to do with her? How can I explain? She has all her father's documents and all the facts I tried to keep away from her all these years."

Maya sat on the bed, feeling abandoned. Her mind couldn't rest, thinking about her daughter and the ominous decision she spoke of. Maya's children were more precious to her than anything else in life, and now the bond with her oldest child was broken because. *She knows the truth about their father. Soon Anika will know too. I can't reverse this chain of events.*

Maya jumped from her bed and went to Anika's bedroom door. She stood gazing at Anika's sleeping face, knowing that she'd lost her trust forever.

And as Maya tried to fall asleep she started thinking about David, and what sort of a man he was. How had this affliction come upon her again after so many years of him being out of their lives? David had been an ordinary individual. He wasn't wealthy, strong, or handsome. Not the man she wished she'd married. On the other hand, he had been quite a good provider. He went to work regularly and made a decent living. He willingly spent his salary for his family's upkeep and for my needs.

He took care of the children and always vacationed with the family. He never looked at other women and was loyal. Being a father filled him with joy. Maya remembered that when first she told him she was pregnant, he had made no fuss about this sudden announcement, and had immediately offered to marry her.

Afterwards, when he learned about her immigration status and the various issues regarding associated with it, he proved his goodness and offered all his help to correct things. After so many years of being alone, Maya realized that her dream of a prince in shining armor would never materialize. Perhaps she'd been married to one, not a prince precisely, but a good man.

The next morning Maya opened her eyes wide as she heard a knock on her bedroom door. There was a pause and Maya then heard the knocking again. The door opened quietly and Ally walked into the bedroom, walking as though she were carrying a heavy weight.

"Mother, I'm leaving for Toronto. I'm going to Uncle's place. I spoke with him yesterday and he told me that both Anika and I have saving trusts established by our father and his family available to us," Ally said.

"Damn it, Ally! What are you doing? You're supposed to start college soon."

"No more of this, Mother. I'm going to reunite with my father's family. I was isolated from them for too long. I want to learn more about Dad. I'll be going to school in Canada now. Perhaps I'll come to see you at Christmas. I'll also expect you to send Anika to visit me several times a year. I hope you won't object to these visits or cause any problems. "

"What are you doing, Ally?"

"Let me alone, Mother. I'm sick of listening to your nonsense about my father and my father's family. I'm going to correct this."

"Ally, wait a bit. I'll help you understand those documents. You'll see them for the farce they are then. If you go away now I'm afraid I'll never see you again!"

"Good-bye, Mother! I'll call Anika as much as I can. Please don't block my phone calls like you did with our dad."

Maya lay on the bed muttering to herself, "It's all a whim. Something to do in the moment, but as soon as you need money, then you'll be back. Money is the great power. You'll see."

At that moment Ally heard the taxi driver impatiently blowing the horn, then she rushed through the door carrying her heavy duffle bag. She turned back for one last glimpse of her mother, but Maya's bedroom's door was still closed.

APPENDIX

Issues Raised in this Book

The Unjust Legal System

This novel deals with the issue of our unjust legal system, where verdicts should be decided based on evidence and the law, but are heavily influenced by the emotions and prejudices of the judges. In the family law area, federal courts have insisted upon deference to state courts, carving out a kind of "abstention" from domestic matters.

Federal courts have credited state trial courts with having particular authority and expertise to adjudicate family law matters. This family law exception to federal court jurisdiction leaves state family court judges with almost exclusive authority over familial disputes.

State trial judges have almost unlimited authority to shape the lives of a family in distress. The vast majority of these decisions require judges to exercise considerable discretion. In this capacity, state court judges make important value judgments that influence the lives of not only the litigants before them, but also the community at large. This unlimited authority gives unlimited bias authority to biased judges who are the ultimate "eyes and the ears" for decisions and opinions made by the court.

The Role of Generational Abuse and the Costs to Society

If we approach the assumption that both girls and boys live in the same household, and if this household causes psychological disturbances to the children living there, and the household is abusive and doesn't provide good parenting, we can deduct that there are as many disturbed women in society as men emanating from such households. The probability of a girl becoming an abusive adult should match the probability of a boy becoming an abuser because of similar background exposure.

Taking into account the female genetics and physical differences, I can say that the distribution of abusers may not be exactly the same and that there are more abusive men than abusive women. However, disturbed abusive men will find themselves on the other side of the law, go to jail on acts of abuse and violence and will be removed from their children, while abusive women have their time in the family court and end up with the children under their custody. Once this happens they can abuse with impunity.

Disturbed people are not gender specific. The court cannot handle disturbed or vindictive spouses or the actions of men who do not have any chance in the court. Litigating or fighting in court needs to be done in a prescribed and adversarial way, so men take flight. Most men just cannot fight equally and extensively because of the family and VAWA laws and the legal costs, so they may choose flight at some point.

The victims in all of this are the children. They suffer the most because they lose both psychologically and emotionally. The nation on the whole also loses, as evidenced by the youth filling the juvenile facilities and later turning to crime. The states, in turn, pay higher educational costs, higher correctional costs and have to provide extended funds for social services.

If the government wants to reduce crime, violence, poverty, psychological disturbances and social services and police expenses, they need to approach this problem. The long term solution will benefit society as a whole and reduce government expenses arising from this phenomenon.

Domestic Violence and the Victims that include Men

As many as 30% of men suffer from domestic violence and incidence of this domestic violence escalates before divorce is initiated. Information from an uncorroborated publication says about 8,000 men commit suicide in the US because of false domestic violence allegations, some of these men may also suffer from domestic violence themselves.

This interpretation of family violence implies further that women's aggression is a reaction to men's actions toward them, i.e. blaming the victim for his plight. It is argued, for instance, that a wife who beats her husband has herself been beaten and that her violence is the violence of self-defense (Straus and Gelles, 1990; Pagelow, 1985.)

Men gradually succumb to feelings of self-hatred when faced with accusations that they are bad people who must be blamed for what's wrong with the world and who cannot expect to be treated with kindness or consideration (Thomas, 1993).

A woman can abuse a man with impunity, since she knows he'll have little, if any, recourse in the legal system. She also knows that in the event of a breakdown in the relationship, she'll most likely be given custody of the children and can use them as a weapon against her partner.

Further, even men themselves are made to believe they are the villains who do not deserve acknowledgment and remedy. The same legal protections should be applied both to men and women in the form of Symmetrical Retraining Orders.

Free Speech

This novel dealt with subject matter relating to a New York State law suit that was dismissed after a jury trial. The plaintiff's filed a lawsuit in the NYS Supreme Court for $2,500,000 for royalties from a book and defamation, claiming the antagonist is her. This book was based on a manuscript written during therapy sessions and court transcripts that are public domain.

The plaintiff used this manuscript, which she took illegally from the author's computer, in order to stop visitation rights and to humiliate and harass the author. Strangely, five years later, she demanded royalties on the book.

In the closing statements, the author stated the following to the jury: "This isn't a case about me; this is a case about your freedom, because the consequences of this case are, that you could be sued for your blogs, diaries and any painting or art you create. Consequences could lead to many books being removed from the shelves, and the only cable programs one could watch would be the cookery and weather channels. These are the consequences of the onslaught of lawsuits on freedom of speech in the birthplace of free speech."

Following the closing arguments, the Supreme Court Judge of the State of New York immediately dismissed the case.

Fatherless Nation Statistics

- 63% of youth suicides are from fatherless homes (Source: U.S. D.H.H.S., Bureau of the Census)
- 90% of all homeless and runaway children are from fatherless homes
- 85% of all children that exhibit behavioral disorders come from fatherless homes (Source: Center for Disease Control)
- 80% of rapists motivated with displaced anger come from fatherless homes (Source: Criminal Justice & Behavior, Vol. 14, p. 403-26, 1978.)
- 71% of all high school dropouts come from fatherless homes (Source: National Principals Association Report on the State of High Schools.)
- 75% of all adolescent patients in chemical abuse centers come from fatherless homes (Source: Rainbows for all God's Children.)
- 70% of juveniles in state-operated institutions come from fatherless homes (Source: U.S. Dept. of Justice, Special Report, Sept. 1988)
- 85% of all youths sitting in prisons grew up in a fatherless home (Source: Fulton Co. Georgia jail populations, Texas Dept. of Corrections 1992)
- 37.9% of fathers have no access/visitation rights. *(Source: p. 6, col. II, para. 6, lines 4 & 5, Census Bureau P. 60, #173, Sept. 1991.)*
- "40% of mothers reported that they had interfered with the non-custodial father's visitation on at least one occasion, to punish the ex-spouse." *(Source: p. 449, col. II, lines 3-6, (citing Fulton) Frequency of visitation by Divorced Fathers; Differences*

in Reports by Fathers and Mothers. Sanford Braver et al, Am. J. of Orthopsychiatry, 1991.)

- "Overall, approximately 50% of mothers "see no value in the father's continued contact with his children...." (Source: Surviving the Breakup, Joan Kelly & Judith Wallerstein, p. 125)
- Only 11% of mothers value their husband's input when it comes to handling problems with their kids. Teachers & doctors rated 45%, and close friends & relatives rated 16%. (Source: EDK Associates survey of 500 women for Redbook Magazine. Redbook, November 1994, p. 36)
- "The former spouse (mother) was the greatest obstacle to having more frequent contact with the children." (Source: Increasing our understanding of fathers who have infrequent contact with their children, James Dudley, Family Relations, Vol. 4, p. 281, July 1991.)
- "A clear majority (70%) of fathers felt that they had too little time with their children." (Source: Visitation and the Noncustodial Father, Mary Ann Kock & Carol Lowery, Journal of Divorce, Vol. 8, No. 2, p. 54, Winter 1984.)
- "Very few of the children were satisfied with the amount of contact with their fathers, after divorce." (Source: Visitation and the Noncustodial Father, Koch & Lowery, Journal of Divorce and Remarriage, Vol. 8, No. 2, p. 50, Winter 1984.)
- "Feelings of anger towards their former spouses hindered effective involvement on the part of fathers; angry mothers would sometimes sabotage father's efforts to visit their children." (Source: Ahrons and Miller, Am. Journal of Orthopsychiatry, Vol. 63. p. 442, July '93.)
- "Mothers may prevent visits to retaliate against fathers for problems in their marital or post-marital relationship." (Source:

Seltzer, Shaeffer & Charing, Journal of Marriage & the Family, Vol. 51, p. 1015, November 1989.)

- In a study: "Visitational Interference — A National Study" by Ms. J Annette Vanini, M.S.W. and Edward Nichols, M.S.W., it was found that 77% of non-custodial fathers are *not* able to "visit" their children, as ordered by the court, as a result of "visitation interference" perpetuated by the custodial parent. In other words, non-compliance with court ordered visitation is three times the problem of non-compliance with court ordered child support and impacts the children of divorce even more. *(Originally published Sept. 1992.)*

Child Support Stats

- Information from multiple sources show that only 10% of all non-custodial fathers fit the "deadbeat dad" category: 90% of the fathers with joint custody paid the support due. Fathers with visitation rights pay 79.1%; and 44.5% of those with NO visitation rights still financially support their children. *(Source: Census Bureau report. Series P. 23, No. 173).*

- Additionally, of those not paying support, 66% are not doing so because they lack the financial resources to pay *(Source: GAO report: GAO/HRD-92-39 FS).*

- 52% of fathers who owe child support earn less than $6,155 per year. *(Source: The Poverty Studies Institute at the University of Wisconsin, Madison, 1993)*

- 66% of single mothers work less than full time while only 10% of fathers fall into this category. In addition, almost 47% of non-custodial mothers default on support compared with the 27% of fathers who default. *(Source: Garansky and Meyer, DHHS Technical Analysis Paper No. 42, 1991).*

- 66% of all support not paid by non-custodial fathers is due to inability to pay. *(Source: U.S. General Accounting Office Report, GAO/HRD-92-39FS January 1992).*

- Total Custodial Mothers: 11,268,000

  Total Custodial Fathers: 2,907,000 *(Source: Current Population Reports, U.S. Bureau of the Census, Series P. 20, No. 458, 1991).*

- The following is sourced from: Technical Analysis Paper No. 42, U.S. Department of Health and Human Services, Office of Income Security Policy, Oct. 1991, Authors: Meyer and Garansky.

  Custodial mothers who receive a support award: 79.6%

  Custodial fathers who receive a support award: 29.9%

  Non-custodial mothers who totally default on support: 46.9%

  Non-custodial fathers who totally default on support: 26.9%

Facts Regarding False Accusations of Abuse

- 160,000 reports of suspected child abuse were reported in 1963. That number exploded to 1.7 million in 1985.

- There were more than three million reports of alleged child abuse and neglect in 1995. However, two million of those complaints were without foundation or false! *(Source: National Center on Child Abuse and Neglect (NCCAN) Child Maltreatment 1995: Reports From the States to the National Child Abuse and Neglect Data System)*

Fatherless Nation — The Effects

Sexual activity. In a study of 700 adolescents, researchers found that "compared to families with two natural parents living in the home, adolescents from single-parent families have been found to engage in greater and earlier sexual activity."

Source: Carol W. Metzler, et al. "The Social Context for Risky Sexual Behavior Among Adolescents," *Journal of Behavioral Medicine* 17 (1994).

A myriad of maladies. Fatherless children are at a dramatically greater risk of drug and alcohol abuse, mental illness, suicide, poor educational performance, teen pregnancy, and criminality.

Source: U.S. Department of Health and Human Services, National Center for Health Statistics, ***Survey on Child Health***, Washington, DC, 1993.

Drinking problems. Teenagers living in single-parent households are more likely to abuse alcohol and at an earlier age compared to children reared in two-parent households

Source: Terry E. Duncan, Susan C. Duncan and Hyman Hops, "The Effects of Family Cohesiveness and Peer Encouragement on the Development of Adolescent Alcohol Use: A Cohort-Sequential Approach to the Analysis of Longitudinal Data," *Journal of Studies on Alcohol* 55 (1994).

Drug Use: "...the absence of the father in the home affects significantly the behavior of adolescents and results in the greater use of alcohol and marijuana."

Source: Deane Scott Berman, "Risk Factors Leading to Adolescent Substance Abuse," *Adolescence* 30 (1995).

Sexual abuse. A study of 156 victims of child sexual abuse found that the majority of the children came from disrupted or single-parent homes; only 31 percent of the children lived with both biological parents. Although step-families make up only about 10 percent of all families, 27 percent of the abused children lived with either a stepfather or the mother's boyfriend.

Source: Beverly Gomes-Schwartz, Jonathan Horowitz, and Albert P. Cardarelli, "Child Sexual Abuse Victims and Their Treatment," U.S. Department of Justice, Office of Juvenile Justice and Delinquency Prevention.

Child Abuse. Researchers in Michigan determined that "49 percent of all child abuse cases are committed by single mothers."

Source: Joan Ditson and Sharon Shay, "A Study of Child Abuse in Lansing, Michigan," *Child Abuse and Neglect,* 8 (1984).

Deadly predictions. A family structure index — a composite index based on the annual rate of children involved in divorce and the percentage of families with children present that are female-headed — is a strong predictor of suicide among young adult and adolescent white males.

Source: Patricia L. McCall and Kenneth C. Land, "Trends in White Male Adolescent, Young-Adult and Elderly Suicide: Are There Common Underlying Structural Factors?" *Social Science Research* 23, 1994.

High risk. Fatherless children are at dramatically greater risk of suicide.

Source: U.S. Department of Health and Human Services, National Center for Health Statistics, *Survey on Child Health,* Washington, DC, 1993.

Suicidal Tendencies. In a study of 146 adolescent friends of 26 adolescent suicide victims, teens living in single-parent families are not only more likely to commit suicide but also more likely to suffer from psychological disorders, when compared to teens living in intact families.

Source: David A. Brent, et al. "Post-traumatic Stress Disorder in Peers of Adolescent Suicide Victims: Predisposing Factors and Phenomenology." *Journal of the American Academy of Child and Adolescent Psychiatry* 34, 1995.

Confused identities. Boys who grow up in father-absent homes are more likely that those in father-present homes to have trouble establishing appropriate sex roles and gender identity.

Source: P.L. Adams, J.R. Milner, and N.A. Schrepf, *Fatherless Children*, New York, Wiley Press, 1984.

Psychiatric Problems. In 1988, a study of preschool children admitted to New Orleans hospitals as psychiatric patients over a 34-month period found that nearly 80 percent came from fatherless homes.

Source: Jack Block, et al. "Parental Functioning and the Home Environment in Families of Divorce," *Journal of the American Academy of Child and Adolescent Psychiatry*, 27 (1988).

Emotional distress. Children living with a never-married mother are more likely to have been treated for emotional problems.

Source: L. Remez, "Children Who Don't Live with Both Parents Face Behavioral Problems," *Family Planning Perspectives* (January/February 1992).

Uncooperative kids. Children reared by a divorced or never-married mother are less cooperative and score lower on tests of intelligence than children reared in intact families. Statistical analysis of the behavior and intelligence of these children revealed "significant detrimental effects" of living in a female-headed household. Growing up in a female-headed household remained a statistical predictor of behavior problems even after adjusting for differences in family income.

Source: Greg L. Duncan, Jeanne Brooks-Gunn and Pamela Kato Klebanov, "Economic Deprivation and Early Childhood Development," *Child Development* 65 (1994).

Unstable families, unstable lives. Compared to peers in two-parent homes, black children in single-parent households are more likely to engage in troublesome behavior, and perform poorly in school.

Source: Tom Luster and Hariette Pipes McAdoo, "Factors Related to the Achievement and Adjustment of Young African-American Children." *Child Development* 65 (1994): 1080-1094.

Beyond class lines. Even controlling for variations across groups in parent education, race and other child and family factors, 18- to 22-year-olds from disrupted families were twice as likely to have poor relationships with their mothers and fathers, to show high levels of emotional distress or problem behavior, [and] to have received psychological help.

Source: Nicholas Zill, Donna Morrison, and Mary Jo Coiro, "Long Term Effects of Parental Divorce on Parent-Child Relationships, Adjustment and Achievement in Young Adulthood." *Journal of Family Psychology* 7 (1993).

Fatherly influence. Children with fathers at home tend to do better in school, are less prone to depression and are more successful in relationships. Children from one-parent families achieve less and get into trouble more than children from two parent families.

Source: *One Parent Families and Their Children: The School's Most Significant Minority,* conducted by The Consortium for the Study of School Needs of Children from One Parent Families, co-sponsored by the National Association of Elementary School Principals and the Institute for Development of Educational Activities, a division of the Charles F. Kettering Foundation, Arlington, VA., 1980.

Divorce disorders. Children whose parents separate are significantly more likely to engage in early sexual activity, abuse drugs, and experience conduct and mood disorders. This effect is especially strong for children whose parents separated when they were five years old or younger.

Source: David M. Fergusson, John Horwood and Michael T. Lynsky, "Parental Separation, Adolescent Psychopathology, and Problem Behaviors," *Journal of the American Academy of Child and Adolescent Psychiatry* 33 (1944).

Troubled marriages, troubled kids. Compared to peers living with both biological parents, sons and daughters of divorced or separated parents exhibited significantly more conduct problems. Daughters of divorced or separated mothers showed significantly higher rates of internalizing problems, such as anxiety or depression.

Source: Denise B. Kandel, Emily Rosenbaum and Kevin Chen, "Impact of Maternal Drug Use and Life Experiences on Preadolescent Children Born to Teenage Mothers," *Journal of Marriage and the Family* 56 (1994).

Hungry for love. "Father hunger" often afflicts boys age one and two whose fathers are suddenly and permanently absent. Sleep disturbances, such as trouble falling asleep, nightmares, and night terrors frequently begin within one to three months after the father leaves home.

Source: Alfred A. Messer, "Boys Father Hunger: The Missing Father Syndrome," *Medical Aspects of Human Sexuality,* January 1989.

Disturbing news: Children of never-married mothers are more than twice as likely to have been treated for an emotional or behavioral problem.

Source: U.S. Department of Health and Human Services, National Center for Health Statistics, *National Health Interview Survey*, Hyattsille, MD, 1988.

Poor and in trouble: A 1988 Department of Health and Human Services study found that at every income level except the very highest (over $50,000 a year), children living with never-married mothers were more likely than their counterparts in two-parent families to have been expelled or suspended from school, to display emotional problems, and to engage in antisocial behavior.

Source: James Q. Wilson, "In Loco Parentis: Helping Children When Families Fail Them," *The Brookings Review*, Fall 1993.

Fatherless aggression: In a longitudinal study of 1,197 fourth-grade students, researchers observed "greater levels of aggression in boys from mother-only households than from boys in mother-father households."

Source: N. Vaden-Kierman, N. Ialongo, J. Pearson, and S. Kellam, "Household Family Structure and Children's Aggressive Behavior: A Longitudinal Study of Urban Elementary School Children," *Journal of Abnormal Child Psychology* 23, no. 5 (1995).

Act now, pay later: "Children from mother-only families have less of an ability to delay gratification and poorer impulse control (that is, control over anger and sexual gratification.) These children also have a weaker sense of conscience or sense of right and wrong."

Source: E.M. Hetherington and B. Martin, "Family Interaction" in H.C. Quay and J.S. Werry (eds.), *Psychopathological Disorders of Childhood.* (New York: John Wiley & Sons, 1979).

Crazy victims: Eighty percent of adolescents in psychiatric hospitals come from broken homes.

Source: J.B. Elshtain, "Family Matters...," Christian Century, July 1993.

Duh to dead: "The economic consequences of a [father's] absence are often accompanied by psychological consequences, which include higher-than-average levels of youth suicide, low intellectual and education performance, and higher-than-average rates of mental illness, violence and drug use."

Source: William Galston, Elaine Kamarck. Progressive Policy Institute. 1993.

Expelled: Nationally, 15.3 percent of children living with a never-married mother and 10.7 percent of children living with a divorced mother have been expelled or suspended from school, compared to only 4.4 percent of children living with both biological parents.

Source: Debra Dawson, "Family Structure...," Journal of Marriage and Family, No. 53. 1991.

Violent rejection: Kids who exhibited violent behavior at school were 11 times as likely not to live with their fathers and six times as likely to have parents who were not married. Boys from families with absent fathers are at higher risk for violent behavior than boys from intact families.
Source: J.L. Sheline (et al.), "Risk Factors...," American Journal of Public Health, No. 84. 1994.

That crowd: Children without fathers or with stepfathers were less likely to have friends who think it's important to behave properly in school. They also exhibit more problems with behavior and in achieving goals.
Source: Nicholas Zill, C. W. Nord, "Running in Place," Child Trends, Inc. 1994.

Likeliest to succeed: Kids who live with both biological parents at age 14 are significantly more likely to graduate from high school than those kids who live with a single parent, a parent and step-parent, or neither parent.
Source: G.D. Sandefur (et al.), "The Effects of Parental Marital Status...," *Social Forces*, September 1992.

Worse to bad: Children in single-parent families tend to score lower on standardized tests and to receive lower grades in school. Children in single-parent families are nearly twice as likely to drop out of school as children from two-parent families.
Source: J.B. Stedman (et al.), "Dropping Out," Congressional Research Service Report No 88-417. 1988.

College odds: Children from disrupted families are 20 percent more unlikely to attend college than kids from intact, two-parent families.
Source: J. Wallerstein, Family Law Quarterly, 20. (Summer 1986).

On their own: Kids living in single-parent homes or in step-families report lower educational expectations on the part of their parents, less parental monitoring of school work, and less overall social supervision than children from intact families.

Source: N.M. Astore and S. McLanahan, *American Sociological Review*, No. 56 (1991).

Double-risk: Fatherless children — kids living in homes without a stepfather or without contact with their biological father — are twice as likely to drop out of school.

Source: U.S. Dept. of Health and Human Services, *Survey on Child Health.* (1993).

Repeat, repeat: Nationally, 29.7 percent of children living with a never-married mother and 21.5 percent of children living with a divorced mother have repeated at least one grade in school, compared to 11.6 percent of children living with both biological parents.

Source: Debra Dawson, "Family Structure and Children's Well-Being," Journals of Marriage and Family, No. 53. (1991).

Underpaid high achievers: Children from low-income, two-parent families outperform students from high-income, single-parent homes. Almost twice as many high achievers come from two-parent homes as one-parent homes.

Source: "One-Parent Families and Their Children;" Charles F. Kettering Foundation (1990).

Dadless and dumb: At least one-third of children experiencing a parental separation "demonstrated a significant decline in academic performance" persisting at least three years.

Source: L.M.C. Bisnairs (et al.), *American Journal of Orthopsychiatry*, no. 60 (1990).

Son of Solo: According to a recent study of young, non-custodial fathers who are behind on child support payments, less than half of these men were living with their own father at age 14.

Slip-sliding: Among black children between the ages of 6 to 9 years old, black children in mother-only households scored significantly lower on tests of intellectual ability, than black children living with two parents.
Source: Luster and McAdoo, *Child Development* 65. 1994.

Dadless dropouts: After taking into account race, socioeconomic status, sex, age and ability, high school students from single-parent households were 1.7 times more likely to drop out than were their corresponding counterparts living with both biological parents.
Source: Ralph McNeal, *Sociology of Education* 88. 1995.

Takes two: Families in which both the child's biological or adoptive parents are present in the household show significantly higher levels of parental involvement in the child's school activities than do mother-only families or step-families.
Source: Zill and Nord, "Running in Place." Child Trends. 1994

Con garden: Forty-three percent of prison inmates grew up in a single-parent household — 39 percent with their mothers, 4 percent with their fathers — and an additional 14 percent lived in households without either biological parent. Another 14 percent had spent at last part of their childhood in a foster home, agency or other juvenile institution.
Source: US Bureau of Justice Statistics, Survey of State Prison Inmates. 1991.

Criminal moms, criminal kids: The children of single teenage mothers are more at risk for later criminal behavior. In the case of a teenage mother, the absence of a father also increases the risk of harshness from the mother.
Source: M. Mourash, L. Rucker, *Crime and Delinquency* 35. 1989.

Rearing rapists: Seventy-two percent of adolescent murderers grew up without fathers. Sixty percent of America's rapists grew up the same way.

Source: D. Cornell (et al.), *Behavioral Sciences and the Law*, 5. 1987. And N. Davidson, "Life Without Father," *Policy Review*. 1990.

Crime and poverty: The proportion of single-parent households in a community predicts its rate of violent crime and burglary, but the community's poverty level doesn't.

Source: D.A. Smith and G.R. Jarjoura, "Social Structure and Criminal Victimization," *Journal of Research in Crime and Delinquency* 25. 1988.

Marriage matters: Only 13 percent of juvenile delinquents come from families in which the biological mother and father are married to each other. By contract, 33 percent have parents who are either divorced or separated and 44 percent have parents who were never married.

Source: Wisconsin Dept. of Health and Social Services, April 1994.

No good time: Compared to boys from intact, two-parent families, teenage boys from disrupted families are not only more likely to be incarcerated for delinquent offenses, but also to manifest worse conduct while incarcerated.

Source: M Eileen Matlock et al., "Family Correlates of Social Skills..." *Adolescence* 29. 1994.

Count 'em: Seventy percent of juveniles in state reform institutions grew up in single- or no-parent situations.

Source: Alan Beck et al., *Survey of Youth in Custody, 1987*, US Bureau of Justice Statistics, 1988.

The Main Thing: The relationship between family structure and crime is so strong that controlling for family configuration erases the relationship between race and crime and between low income and crime. This conclusion shows up time and again in the literature.

Source: E. Kamarck, William Galston, *Putting Children First*, Progressive Policy Inst. 1990.

Examples: Teenage fathers are more likely than their childless peers to commit and be convicted of illegal activity, and their offenses are of a more serious nature.

Source: M.A. Pirog-Good, "Teen Father and the Child Support System," in *Paternity Establishment*, Institute for research on Poverty, Univ. of Wisconsin. 1992.

The 'hood The likelihood that a young male will engage in criminal activity doubles if he's raised without a father and triples if he lives in a neighborhood with a high concentration of single-parent families.

Source: A. Anne Hill, June O'Neill, "Underclass Behaviors in the United States," CUNY, Baruch College. 1993.

Bringing the war back home The odds that a boy born in America in 1974 will be murdered are higher than the odds that a serviceman in World War II would be killed in combat.

Source: US Sen. Phil Gramm, 1995.

Get ahead at home and at work: Fathers who cared for their children intellectual development and their adolescent's social development were more like to advance in their careers, compared to men who weren't involved in such activities.

Source: J. Snarey, *How Fathers Care for the Next Generation*. Harvard Univ. Press.

Diaper dads: In 1991, about 20 percent of preschool children were cared for by their fathers — both married and single. In 1988, the number was 15 percent.

Source: M. O'Connell, "Where's Papa? Father's Role in Child Care," Population Reference Bureau. 1993.

Without leave: Sixty-three percent of 1500 CEOs and human resource directors said it wasn't reasonable for a father to take a leave after the birth of a child.

Source: J.H. Pleck, "Family Supportive Employer Policies," Center for research in Women. 1991.

Get a job: The number of men who complain that work conflicts with their family responsibilities rose from 12 percent in 1977 to 72 percent in 1989. Meanwhile, 74 percent of men prefer a "daddy track" job to a "fast track" job.

Source: James Levine, The Fatherhood Project.

Long-distance dads: Twenty-six percent of absent fathers live in a different state than their children.

Source: US Bureau of the Census, *Statistical Brief*. 1991.

Cool Dad of the Week: Among fathers who maintain contact with their children after a divorce, the pattern of the relationship between father-and-child changes. They begin to behave more like relatives than like parents. Instead of helping with homework, nonresident dads are more likely to take the kids shopping, to the movies, or out to dinner. Instead of providing steady advice and guidance, divorced fathers become "treat dads."

Source: F. Furstenberg, A. Cherlin, *Divided Families*. Harvard Univ. Press. 1991.

Older is not wiser: While 57 percent of unwed dads with kids no older than two visit their children more than once a week, by the time the kid's seven and a half, only 23 percent are in frequent contact with their children.

Source: R. Lerman and Theodora Ooms, *Young Unwed Fathers*. 1993.

Ten years after: Ten years after the breakup of a marriage, more than two-thirds of kids report not having seen their father for a year.

Source: National Commission on Children, *Speaking of Kids*. 1991.

No such address: More than half the kids who don't live with their father have never been in their father's house.

Source: F. Furstenberg, A. Cherlin, Divided Families. Harvard Univ. Press. 1991.

Dadless years: About 40 percent of the kids living in fatherless homes haven't seen their dads in a year or more. Of the rest, only one in five sleeps even one night a month at the father's home. And only one in six sees their father once or more per week.

Source: F. Furstenberg, A. Cherlin, Divided Families. Harvard Univ. Press. 1991.

Measuring up? According to a 1992 Gallup poll, more than 50 percent of all adults agreed that fathers today spend less time with their kids than their fathers did with them.

Source: Gallup national random sample conducted for the National Center for Fathering, April 1992.

Father unknown. Of kids living in single-mom households, 35 percent never see their fathers, and another 24 percent see their fathers less than once a month.

Source: J.A. Selzer, "Children's Contact with Absent Parents," Journal of Marriage and the Family, 50 (1988).

Missed contact: In a study of 304 young adults, those whose parents divorced after they left home had significantly less contact with their fathers than adult children who parents remained married. Weekly contact with their children dropped from 78 percent for still-married fathers to 44 percent for divorced fathers.

Source: William Aquilino, "Later Life Parental Divorce and Widowhood," Journal of Marriage and the Family 56. 1994.

Commercial breaks: The amount of time a father spends with his child — one-on-one — averages less than 10 minutes a day.

Source: J. P. Robinson, et al., "The Rhythm of Everyday Life." Westview Press. 1988

High risk: Overall, more than 75 percent of American children are at risk because of paternal deprivation. Even in two-parent homes, fewer than 25 percent of young boys and girls experience an average of at least one hour a day of relatively individualized contact with their fathers.

Source: Henry Biller, "The Father Factor..." a paper based on presentations during meetings with William Galston, Deputy Director, Domestic Policy, Clinton White House, December 1993 and April 1994.

Knock, knock: Of children age 5 to 14, 1.6 million return home to houses where there is no adult present.

Source: U.S. Bureau of the Census, "Who's Minding the Kids?" Statistical Brief. April 1994.

Who said talk's cheap? Almost 20 percent of sixth- through twelfth-graders haven't had a good conversation lasting for at least 10 minutes with at least one of their parents in more than a month.

Source: Peter Benson, "The Troubled Journey." Search Institute. 1993.

Justified guilt. A 1990 L.A. Times poll found that 57 percent of all fathers and 55 percent of all mothers feel guilty about not spending enough time with their children.

Source: Lynn Smith and Bob Sipchen, "Two Career Family Dilemma," Los Angeles Times, Aug. 12, 1990.

Who are you, mister? In 1965, parents on average spent approximately 30 hours a week with their kids. By 1985, the amount of time had fallen to 17 hours.

Source: William Mattox, "The Parent Trap." Policy Review. Winter, 1991.

Waiting Works: Only eight percent of those who finished high school, got married before having a child, and waited until age 20 to have that child were living in poverty in 1992.

Source: William Galston, "Beyond the Murphy Brown Debate." Institute for Family Values. Dec. 10, 1993.

www.ingramcontent.com/pod-product-compliance
Lightning Source LLC
Chambersburg PA
CBHW052023070526
44584CB00016B/1878